RIBS

RIBS

With Low & Slow BBQ Guide

ADAM ROBERTS

NEW
HOLLAND

For Kristy, Jackson and Paige — you guys are my world.

CONTENTS

ABOUT THE BOOK

RIBS is a culmination of the very best tips, techniques and secret recipes from more than twenty years in the kitchen and will sharply improve your rib cooking skills and social standing amongst your friends, family and guests.

This book will take you on a journey of simple recipes, revealing complex flavors and amazing textures. Adam will introduce you to a range of cooking techniques that you can use both in your indoor and outdoor kitchens using a range of common fuels such as charcoal, direct heat and frying oil.

RIBS is your 'go-to' book for not only flavors and textures but also charcoal and wood pairings for superior dishes.

RIBS will help beginners master a range of barbecue and grilling techniques and uses modern kitchen appliances, giving a budding 'Rib King' a fighting chance in case of a rainy day or restricted cooking space.

Not all recipes are going to take hours to knock together—Adam has included some finger lickin' hot and fast rib recipes to make watching your next footy game so much more tasty.

RIBS contains recipes for all levels of ability and with the easy to follow instructions, you'll have plenty of fun learning new ways to wow your friends and family with the perfect ribs for any occasion.

OUTDOOR KITCHEN

Cooking over fire and burning wood and charcoal has been around since the birth of man and continues to be one of the most exciting ways to cook a meal.

There are many outdoor kitchens in modern society and plenty of variations of grills, barbecues, smokers and ovens. Let's take a look at some of the more common options.

OUTDOOR KITCHEN COOKERS

Bullet-shaped Smoker

These have a fire basket at the bottom under a water pan with two grill plate stackers on top for versatility. Usually made from a porcelain-coated mild steel. Lightweight and easy to transport.

Pizza Oven

They come in many shapes and sizes and usually have the fire in a separate chamber or off to the back or side. Normally set in place and quite hard to move around.

Egg-shaped Grill

The quality units are made from a ceramic shell, with the fire plate on the inside of the main chamber. It has a solid construction and while not overly easy to transport it is easy to move around if on wheels.

Offset Smoker

You get what you pay for more than any other barbecue with offset smokers. Some of the cheaper units will have thinner steel construction and can be much more difficult to keep at a stable temperature. The firebox is usually 'set off to the side' of the main chamber, which is where it gets the name 'offset'.

Electric Smoker

Considered one of the easiest barbecue smokers to use. Most come with a digital display or easy selector switch option panel to increase or decrease temperature with ease as well as an option to produce smoke at will. Fuelled by automatically fed wood pellets designed specifically for the unit.

Kettle Barbecue

The old faithful. The fire plate or cradle is inside the unit with little space between fire and food. Fire can be set off to one side of the unit for indirect cooking and the use of a 'snake' of briquettes can prevent the unit from overheating or to keep the temperature stable.

Featured Barbecue

In this book, I've chosen one of the more versatile and easy to use outdoor grills to keep it simple, in case you've never tried using flame or coals for cooking. For the seasoned barbecuers, feel free to use your own barbecue or grill and simply use my methods and recipes as a guide.

The barbecue I have used for this book is the versatile egg-shaped ceramic shell smoker, known as a Kamado or simply as an Egg. There are several major brands of this style of unit found across the globe including Primo, the Big Green Egg and the Kamado Joe.

I often cook on many different types of barbecues including a bullet-shaped smoker, rotisserie spit, offset smoker and pizza oven but I find the ceramic egg smoker particularly easy to cook up some amazing ribs.

The versatility of the 'Egg' is a key factor as it can grill, hot smoke and bake depending on how you configure the unit. These units can vary in price from entry level to the highest quality of fabrication. Do your research on any barbecue smoker as quite often you get what you pay for.

OUTDOOR KITCHEN TECHNIQUES

Indirect Hot Smoking

This method is also known as 'low 'n' slow' barbecuing and can take a decent amount of cooking time. The term low and slow simply means cooking meats at low temperatures for a long period of time. This method undoubtedly delivers the best flavor and textural results and is definitely worth the wait.

Indirect hot smoking involves placing the meat inside the barbecue smoker away from the heat source, or out of the way of the 'direct' heat. It also promotes the use of smoking woods or chips to impart flavors into the meat as it cooks. This method can often produce a visually appealing 'smoke ring' around the meat on some quality barbecue units.

Grilling

Grilling is simply placing the meat directly over the heat source which allows the meat to cook 'hot and fast' and can often be a great way to speed up a cook and still impart some smoky goodness into the meat if using the right charcoals.

Roasting

This method is exactly how it reads and is pretty much doing the same job as your indoor oven except that you're using wood or charcoal as your main heat source instead of electricity.

With this method, you'll no doubt be using the 'indirect' method of cooking, ensuring the food is placed away from the direct heat to produce the best results.

The use of deflector plates is a good way to prevent direct grilling and are a key feature of the Egg-style barbecue unit.

UELS & SMOKING WOODS

Types of smoking woods and the best fuels to use will create debate wherever you are across the globe. Below is a simple guide as a starting point.

Charcoal Briquette

Charcoal briquettes are excellent for many reasons and are suited to some barbecues or grills more than others. Essentially, they're easy to light, lightweight and can be stored quite easily. They're available at a whole range of different stockists, from corner stores to large chain supermarkets and everywhere in between.

One of my preferred briquettes is the Kingsford applewood infused briquettes which have small chips of smoking wood infused in the briquette and give off plenty of flavor.

There are various shapes, compounds and ingredients used in the range of briquettes in any marketplace. I personally prefer to stick to the natural products and products that use minimal binding chemicals or additives to ensure these elements don't interfere with the flavors I'm working hard to achieve.

Lump Charcoal

Lump charcoal is essentially lumps of charcoal that have been processed from real pieces of wood and look just like a piece of timber that's already been burned.

The lump charcoal often burns hotter than most briquettes and is great for mid-sized barbecue grills and upwards and is a great fuel to use for direct grilling.

I like to use a combination of predominantly the wood chip infused briquettes and a few pieces of lump charcoal to give me a stable heat and a quality smoke or burn. I also find this flavors the meats just right without over-smoking.

Hardwoods

There are many varieties of hardwoods which can be great for heat and smoke and the use of hardwoods are usually set aside for the larger of the barbecue grills like your offset smokers.

Common hardwoods such as mesquite, hickory, ironbark and black wattle are common in both the United States and Australia but each country is going to have a native equivalent which I am certain will do the job.

What you're looking for in a hardwood is something that has been seasoned (or dried) and has a low moisture content, to ensure a clean burn and a clean smoke.

There's nothing worse than throwing a moist piece of wood on the fire and seeing white billowing smoke coming out the chimney. Not only does this smell quite acrid and much like a campfire, it can seriously ruin a perfectly good cook inside the barbecue smoker.

Lighting the Fire

The use of a chimney starter will make life very easy when getting your fire going. I recommend using a chimney starter for every type of barbecue, grill or smoker and fully lighting your briquettes or charcoal before placing them into your fire chamber.

In the bottom of the chimney, simply place your preferred fire-starting cube or tablet and pour your briquettes, lump charcoal or small kindling wood on top and set that baby on fire. Be sure to place the lit chimney starter on a surface that can take heat such as a concrete pad, brick stack or pavers.

Some people don't mind using fire lighting kindling or easy light starters inside their barbecue or firebox but I'd rather keep the chemicals outside of the unit, and only feed my rigs with quality and all-natural fuels.

Smoking Technique

Hot smoking is nowhere near as tricky as it may first seem. You simply light your fuel, add a few chips, chunks or pieces on top of the fuel and you have smoke.

Where the complexity may come into play with hot smoking is in choosing the right type of smoking woods for your particular barbecue or grill and also pairing with your food to achieve the best results.

I've found a happy place in ensuring I only pair light proteins with light-flavored woods and reserve the heavier woods for heavier cuts of meat.

Feel free to try the following suggestions:

Chicken & Pork = Fruit woods, pecan wood
Lamb & Beef = Hardwoods, hickory, mesquite, ironbark, black wattle

BARBECUE & WOOD PAIRINGS

Egg-shaped Barbecue
Fuel: Briquettes and/or lump charcoal
Wood: Chips, small chunks or infused briquettes
Uses: Hot smoking, grilling and roasting/baking

Offset Smoker
Fuel: Seasoned hardwood, lump charcoal
Wood: Hardwood logs, chunks of fruit wood
Uses: Hot smoking

Kettle
Fuel: Briquettes and/or lump charcoal
Wood: Chips, small chunks or infused briquettes
Uses: Hot smoking, grilling and roasting/baking

Bullet-shaped Smoker
Fuel: Briquettes and/or lump charcoal
Wood: Chips, small chunks or infused briquettes
Uses: Cold smoking, hot smoking, grilling, roasting baking

Electric
Fuel: Electricity and in some units, wood pellets
Wood: Flavored pellets
Uses: Hot Smoking

SMOKE

Over-smoking the meat is a common mistake when hot smoking. For best results, ensure that your smoker and wood fuel or smoking woods or chips burn with a clean light or thin blue smoke plume.

With most cuts of meat, you won't need a lot of smoking chips or chunks to produce a subtle smoky flavor. With the smaller to medium-sized barbecue units, a couple of handfuls of chips or a couple of small logs of fruitwood (approx. 20 cm x 4 cm/8 in x 1½ in) placed in the unit after the fuel is going will give you plenty of smoke and most likely a great flavor result.

To ensure that you don't over-smoke too early, space the addition of smoking wood or chips out into intervals, placing one handful or chunk at a time and let it burn through. Give it a few more minutes and then add the second batch and so on until you use up your desired amount of smoking wood.

You can do some research more specifically on at what internal temperatures a particular protein will stop taking in smoke. There's plenty of information out there on that topic in particular.

If I am hot smoking or low 'n' slow barbecuing, I usually ensure that I have a constant flow of clean smoke working through the unit for the first hour to hour and a half for a longer cook of 3 or more hours. For shorter cooks and lighter meats such as chicken and pork, I normally just use a handful or two of wood chips or small chunks total which I find is plenty.

Grilling and barbecuing is all about having fun and experimenting so play around with the quantities and flavors of the smoking woods to suit your personal taste.

Internal Temperatures

You will often hear the phrase, 'cook to temp not to time' among a lot of low 'n' slow barbecuers around the world. This is certainly very true and a great way to learn when a protein is ready for consumption.

Many folks use a digital thermometer or probe which will give an internal temperature reading once the probe is placed into the meat.

The discussion around what the optimum internal temperature of a particular cut of meat should be is somewhat subjective, depending on how you like the texture of your food. Some of us love a medium-rare steak over a well-done steak so the internal temperature that one prefers is going to vary, obviously.

With low 'n' slow barbecuing, I cook to both temperature and time but also sight and feel. This can sound a bit daunting but I'll explain the concept.

When I'm cooking for a specific meal or gathering, I'm usually cooking to a particular time. I'll allow myself a good solid window with which to cook the meats and work back from the desired 'plate up' target.

I will often check the meat with a digital thermometer to check on progress and to see where the internal temperature of the meat is at, keeping in mind the approximate 'finish' temp that I am aiming for. I'll calculate how long the meat has taken to get to the current internal temperature and estimate how much time I have left at the current ambient barbecue temperature until I should reach the finish line.

If for some reason the protein isn't cooking as fast as I would like, I add some more fuel to the fire and effectively turn the heat up a bit to bring the meat up to speed. I'm very careful to only increase the heat by small increments as I don't want to overcook the meat, or finish too early.

Cooking to sight also comes into play when I'm nearing the end of the cook when I'm looking to see a nice color on the meat and it essentially looks like it is ready for the plate. After many barbecues, you'll soon learn what a cooked protein looks like and it will become a great indicator to prepare for serving up.

Feeling the meat can be done in a number of ways to check if it is cooked. I use a temperature probe and probe the meat to feel for resistance in the meat. With most low 'n' slow cook ups, I'm aiming for a super-tender texture of the meat and when I probe the meat, I'm looking for minimal resistance or even none at all.

INDOOR KITCHEN

For cleaner cooking compared to the outdoor kitchen, it's hard to go past cooking techniques that use everyday appliances in your indoor kitchen.

In this book I've stuck to a few old faithful methods and processes so as not to lose you with anything too fancy. After all, this book is more about producing excellent food not mastering dozens of different appliances.

Grill Pan

The heavier gauge steel, the better for your go-to grill pan. If your grill pan is made of good-quality steel to start with, you'll have very few problems with it across a lifetime. Keep the grill pan well-seasoned and please don't ever, ever put it in the dishwasher.

In this book I've stuck to using the grill pan on the stovetop which can be over gas or electric but feel free to challenge yourself by using it in conjunction with your campfire coals or on the barbecue.

As a general rule, always keep a fire blanket or kitchen specific fire extinguisher handy at all times whilst cooking with hot oil. You never know when you're going to need it. For maximum safety, never leave frying oil unattended whilst it is cooking.

With my grill pan, I like to bring the temperature up gradually and cook over a medium heat for most dishes. This ensures I'm not burning something on the outside and having a raw finish on the inside.

Pressure Cooker

What a fantastic piece of kit this is for the indoor kitchen. Take your heavier cuts of meat and turn them into moist and tender morsels in minutes.

Most large chain stores have a decent range of these appliances. I'd be going for a multi-function unit that slow cooks, pressure cooks and keeps food warm for maximum flexibility. They're simple to use and normally have a range of settings at the push of a button.

In this book I've concentrated on the pressure cooking to speed up the cook process as the outdoor kitchen has quite a few low 'n' slow techniques which I find produce a much better 'slow cooked' result.

Benchtop Deep-Fryer

Having spent some of my early cooking years behind the commercial version of the deep-fryer, I simply cannot do without one of these on my kitchen benchtop at home.

The deep-fryer only takes a few minutes to heat up and a few more minutes to cook. You'll be eating some seriously flavorful dishes or footy snacks in no time at all.

A good habit to get into is to drain the cooking oil of any leftover food crumbs or pieces to ensure that the flavor of your last cook up doesn't interfere with your next.

Once the oil has cooled right down, simply pour the oil into a sieve with a thin layer of paper towel to catch the crumbs. Make sure you clean off the heating element and bottom of the fryer pan to remove anything pooling inside the unit.

I have a general rule that if I can't see through the oil to the bottom of the fryer, the oil needs changing. I like to use a canola oil for deep-frying where possible and I definitely drain off as much oil as I can before serving up deep-fried delights.

RUBS

In this book you will see plenty of references to the use of 'rubs'. Rubs are a common element in adding incredible flavor to meats before, during and after cooking, particularly on the barbecue, grill or smoker.

Each recipe has a list of rub ingredients to get you started. Once you're comfortable with the general concept of using rubs, I would strongly suggest that you take the time to create your own rub and experiment with your own flavor profiles to make each recipe your own.

I love to grind my own spices and find that doing this provides a greater and fresher flavor kick to almost every recipe. Owning your own spice grinder is essential and until you've tried grinding your own spices, you've really been missing out. I've found that a small coffee grinder is as good as anything out there and for a few dollars, it's well worth the investment.

Looking closely at the recipes in this book, I have used freshly cracked black pepper quite a lot as a base for the rubs. Putting it simply, I love a good peppery rub and particularly on anything cooked in or on the barbecue. If you're not so keen, simply pare back the quantities suggested until you find your desired level of pepper flavor.

I use agave sugar for its already powdery consistency and sweet taste. You can substitute this for another white sugar if you are unable to find agave sugar in your local grocery store.

Kosher salt is another key ingredient in my cooking and I find that kosher salt is quite subtle in flavor and not too salty, as some of the more refined salts can be. It also works incredibly well with hot smoking and helps form an eye-catching and protective bark, particularly on beef ribs.

A huge tip is to grind your rub ingredients into a fine blend. You certainly don't need your guests munching back on a large peppercorn or half a spoon of salt or chilli. Fine grinding your rubs will also ensure that you're spreading your flavors across the meats much more evenly.

Don't be afraid to fully coat the ribs with a decent coating of rub as this is where most of your flavor is going to come from. A lighter rub means you'll achieve a lighter flavor as an end result and conversely, a heavier rub usually means much more flavor.

I find that adding pre-ground powders to your pantry can save you plenty of time and it's beneficial to find yourself a good supplier who can provide a great range of spice powders in bulk quantities.

Any rub recipe in this book should be used as a guide but the rub recipes that I've included are there particularly to show you the general quantities and combinations of flavors that I've found work well with the particular cut or protein. I can't stress enough that experimenting with rub ingredients is the way to go.

Everyone's palate is different and when you settle on a great all-purpose rub that all your friends and family enjoy, bottle it and sell it to them to pay for your newfound rib cooking addiction.

PORK RIBS

There are a number of ways to cut pork ribs including St Louis cut, spare ribs and baby back cuts. I personally prefer the baby back style for its size and shape but I'm not overly fussed if my local butcher has either of the cuts as they all taste amazing.

I make sure that the ribs have at least 1–2 cm (½–¾ in) of meat on top of the rib rack, covering the bones. There's nothing worse than grabbing a rack of pork ribs where the butcher has sliced off all the top meat revealing the bones and only leaving the meat in between these shiny bones. These racks are called 'shiners' and they're dead-set rubbish to cook with and a huge waste of time and money.

It may cost a couple of extra dollars but do yourself a favor and find yourself a friendly butcher who knows their way around a decent rib rack and who can prepare you some meaty porkies. You'll never look back.

One of the most important areas of preparation for the pork ribs is in removing the membrane from the underside of the ribs. By removing this membrane, you'll allow better flavor and/or smoke penetration during the cook. And your guests won't be biting down on a chewy or tough piece of waste product.

When smoking pork ribs, I love to use fruit woods which have a subtle flavor so as not to over-smoke them as you could easily do if you use some of the heavier smoking woods such as mesquite, hickory or similar.

It is really important that you use the rib recipes contained in this chapter as a guide, particularly for overall cooking time. If your ribs are extra meaty, obviously they can do with a longer cooking time. Going the other way, if you just can't resist buying a few racks of the shiny bones you unfortunately find on most deli shelves, keep a close eye on them during the cook and reduce the cooking time to suit.

Ensure you properly store the pork ribs in the fridge and cook them up within a few days of purchase. If you're not going to cook them up within a few days, simply freeze them until you're ready, it's not going to do them any harm. Alternatively, vacuum seal the ribs to prolong the fridge life.

Save yourself some frustration by removing the membrane from the underside of the ribs before freezing them and if you want to ensure maximum flavor penetration into the rib meat, vacuum seal the ribs which have been pre-rubbed.

You will notice that in this book, I've not included a recipe that includes boiling the ribs. Even though this is a technique used in a majority of commercial kitchens for its ease and tenderness, I find that boiling the ribs can drain the pork of all that natural flavor and goodness – only to have to lather them up with copious amounts of sauce to add back some flavor. It just doesn't make sense to boil your ribs at home and you'll find plenty of fun and flavor with the techniques in this book.

SPICY APPLE & SALTED CARAMEL PORK RIBS

Prep Time: 10 minutes	Cook Time: 2 hours 40 minutes	Serves 4	Cooker: Barbecue Smoker & Medium Pot	Skill Level: Medium

Method

Combine all of the rub ingredients in a bowl.

Remove the membrane from the underside of the pork ribs and apply a liberal coating of the rub to completely cover all sides of the ribs.

Indirectly hot smoke ribs for 1 hour inside a barbecue smoker at 130°C (250°F) with apple or peach wood chunks or chips.

Remove the ribs from the smoker and drizzle with the honey and sliced butter. Double wrap each rack of ribs in foil and return to the smoker for a further 1½ hours at 130°C (250°F).

Allow the ribs to rest for 10 minutes before slicing.

To make the sauce, heat the sugar in a pot over high heat, stirring constantly until the sugar liquefies. Immediately add small cubes of butter until combined. Slowly add in the cream until combined and allow to boil for about 1 minute, then remove from the heat and stir in the salt. Allow to cool before serving.

Drizzle caramel sauce over ribs to serve.

Tip Serve the ribs with vanilla ice cream, crushed pecans and orange zest for a savory sweet dessert. Add cornbread, biscuit or other sides to your preference.

Ingredients

2 racks pork ribs
2 tablespoons honey
100 g (3½ oz) butter, sliced
sesame seeds, to garnish
finely sliced spring onions (scallions), to garnish

Rub

2 tablespoons brown sugar
2 tablespoons finely chopped extra dried apples
1 tablespoon smoked paprika
1 teaspoon celery powder
1 teaspoon garlic powder
1 teaspoon onion powder
1 teaspoon cinnamon powder
1 teaspoon freshly cracked black pepper, finely ground
1 teaspoon kosher salt

Sauce

1 cup white granulated sugar
½ cup thickened cream
125 g (4½ oz) unsalted butter
½ tablespoon kosher salt

SPICY BARBECUE PORK RIBS WITH SWEET SLAW

▨▨▨▨▨▨▨▨▨▨▨▨▨▨▨▨▨▨▨▨▨▨▨▨▨▨▨▨

Prep Time: 30 minutes	Cook Time: 2 hours 20 minutes	Serves 4	Cooker: Barbecue Smoker	Skill Level: Medium

Method

Combine all of the rub ingredients in a bowl.

Remove the membrane from the underside of the pork ribs and apply a liberal coating of the rub to completely cover all sides of the ribs.

Indirectly hot smoke the ribs for 1 hour inside a barbecue smoker at 130°C (250°F) with apple or peach wood chunks or chips.

Remove the ribs from the smoker and add the butter. Double wrap each rack of ribs in foil and return to the smoker for a further 1 hour at 130°C (250°F).

Combine all of the sauce ingredients in a pot, starting with the wet ingredients then the dry ingredients and bring to the boil. Reduce the heat to low and simmer the sauce for 30 minutes. Remove from the heat and allow to cool.

Remove the ribs from the foil and baste the ribs whilst in the smoker with the spicy barbecue sauce twice at 10 minute intervals. Once the second coat of sauce has set, remove and serve with the sweet slaw and extra dipping sauce on the side.

To make the sweet slaw, combine the pears, cabbage, onion and carrot and mix with the sugar, apple cider vinegar and mayonnaise. Serve chilled.

- -

Tip Add or remove quantities of chilli peppers and hot sauce to your preferred heat level.

Ingredients

2 racks (pre-cooked) pork ribs

100 g (3½ oz) butter

Rub

2 tablespoons brown sugar

1 tablespoon smoked paprika

1 teaspoon celery powder

1 teaspoon garlic powder

1 teaspoon onion powder

½ teaspoon Mexican chilli powder

½ teaspoon cayenne pepper

1 tablespoon freshly cracked black pepper, finely ground

1 tablespoon kosher salt

Sauce

250 ml (9 fl oz) tomato sauce (ketchup)

100 ml (3½ fl oz) water

2 tablespoons apple cider vinegar

4 tablespoons brown sugar

3 tablespoons honey

1 teaspoon onion powder

1 teaspoon mustard powder

2 tablespoons hot sauce

1 chipotle pepper, finely diced

1 teaspoon finely ground freshly cracked black pepper

1 teaspoon finely ground kosher salt

Sweet Slaw

2 pears, thinly sliced

½ red cabbage, thinly sliced

½ red onion, thinly sliced

3 carrots, thinly sliced

2 tablespoons white sugar

1 tablespoon apple cider vinegar

3 tablespoons mayonnaise

SMOKED HONEY SESAME PORK RIBS

Prep Time: 10 minutes	Cook Time: 2 hours 40 minutes	Serves 4	Cooker: Barbecue Smoker	Skill Level: Medium

Ingredients

2 racks pork ribs

100 g (3½ oz) honey

100 g (3½ oz) butter, sliced

50 g (1¾ oz) sesame seeds

1 spring onion (scallion), thinly sliced

Rub

2 tablespoons brown sugar

1 tablespoon smoked paprika

1 teaspoon celery powder

1 teaspoon garlic powder

1 teaspoon onion powder

1 tablespoon freshly cracked black pepper, finely ground

1 tablespoon kosher salt

Method

Combine all of the rub ingredients in a bowl.

Remove the membrane from the underside of the pork ribs and apply liberal coating of the rub to completely cover all sides of the ribs.

Indirectly hot smoke the ribs for 1 hour inside a barbecue smoker at 130°C (250°F) with apple or peach wood chunks or chips.

Remove the ribs from the smoker and drizzle with the honey, top with sliced butter. Double wrap each rack of ribs in foil and return to the smoker for a further 1½ hours at 130°C (250°F).

Allow the ribs to rest for 10 minutes before slicing and sprinkling with sesame seeds and spring onion to serve.

Tip Drizzle with extra pre-smoked honey before serving for an extra sweet kick.

PORK RIB & SEAFOOD LAKSA

Prep Time: 25 minutes	Cook Time: 1 hour	Serves 4	Cooker: Pressure Cooker & Grill Pans	Skill Level: Medium

Method

Rub the pork spare ribs with the kosher salt, pepper and smoked paprika. Grill in a pan until well browned.

Add to the pressure cooker with the beef stock, hoisin sauce and red onion and pressure cook for 45 minutes.

Soften the noodles in a bowl of warm water for about 5 minutes and remove to cool.

To make the laksa broth, in a large pan, add the olive oil, laksa paste, beef stock, anchovies, coconut cream, agave sugar and hoisin sauce and bring to the boil. Stir occasionally to ensure ingredients are well combined. Reduce the heat and simmer for a further 20 minutes.

Slice the squid tube into small chunks and add to the laksa along with the finely sliced spring onions and simmer for a further 3 minutes. Remove from the heat to cool slightly.

Remove the pork ribs from the pressure cooker (saving the braising liquid for a stock for another day) and slice into chunks (a small mouthful per chunk).

Shell the prawns and shallow fry in a pan with 2 garlic cloves and 100 g (3½ oz) of butter.

Place the noodles and bean sprouts into each bowl along with sliced pork and two prawns and then pour over laksa broth.

Garnish with lime zest, chilli and coriander to serve.

Tip Add your own favorite seafood chunks instead of prawns or squid.

Ingredients

8 sliced boneless pork spare ribs

1 tablespoon kosher salt

2 tablespoons freshly cracked black pepper

1 tablespoon smoked paprika

100 ml (3½ fl oz) beef stock

1 tablespoon hoisin sauce

½ red onion, finely chopped

250 g (9 oz) vermicelli rice noodles

8 king prawns (jumbo shrimp)

2 garlic cloves

100 g (3½ oz) butter

1 cup bean sprouts

1 tablespoon lime zest, to garnish

1 small red chilli, to garnish

¼ bunch coriander (cilantro), finely chopped, to garnish

Laksa

2 tablespoons olive oil

2 tablespoons laksa paste

375 ml (13 fl oz) beef stock

2 small anchovies

250 ml (9 fl oz) coconut cream

1 tablespoon agave sugar

½ tablespoon hoisin sauce

1 small squid (calamari) tube

½ cup finely sliced spring onion (scallions)

PORK & BRANDY APPLE RIBS WITH STICKY RICE

Prep Time: 20 minutes	Cook Time: 2 hours 40 minutes	Serves 4	Cooker: Barbecue Smoker & Cook Pot	Skill Level: Medium

Method

Combine all of the rub ingredients in a bowl.

Remove the membrane from the underside of the pork ribs and apply a liberal coating of the rub to completely cover all sides of the ribs.

Indirectly hot smoke the ribs for 1 hour inside a barbecue smoker at 130°C (250°F) with apple or peach wood chunks or chips.

Remove the ribs from the smoker and add the sliced butter to the top of the ribs. Individually double-wrap each rack of ribs in foil and return to the smoker meat side down for a further 1½ hours at 130°C (250°F).

To make the sauce, peel and dice the apples and add to a pot of boiling water together with brown sugar and cinnamon and reduce over high heat until the apples are very soft and the liquid has reduced to just cover the apples. Remove from the heat and blend the apples using a blender to form a sauce. Add the brandy to sauce and allow to cool before serving.

Boil the rice to a fluffy consistency and drain the water.

In a mixing bowl, add the sugar and rice wine vinegar to the rice and mix through and garnish with the chilli and mint.

Slice the pork ribs, serve on a bed of fluffy rice and a drizzle of apple sauce.

Ingredients

2 racks pork ribs
100 g (3½ oz) unsalted butter, sliced
400 g (14 oz) white rice
2 tablespoons granular sugar
2 tablespoons rice wine vinegar
1 red chilli, finely sliced
2 mint leaves, to garnish

Rub

2 tablespoons brown sugar
1 tablespoon smoked paprika
1 teaspoon celery powder
1 teaspoon garlic powder
1 teaspoon onion powder
1 tablespoon freshly cracked black pepper, finely ground
1 tablespoon kosher salt

Sauce

4 green apples
500 ml (17 fl oz) water
2 tablespoons brown sugar
1 teaspoon cinnamon
60 ml (2 fl oz) quality brandy

COMPETITION PORK RIBS

Prep Time: 30 minutes	Cook Time: 3 hours	Serves 1 pork rib entry	Cooker: Barbecue Smoker	Skill Level: Expert

Ingredients

2 racks pork ribs

100 g (3½ oz) brown sugar

100 g (3½ oz) unsalted butter

Rub

4 tablespoons pecan powder

2 tablespoons smoked paprika

2 teaspoons garlic powder

2 teaspoons onion powder

1 teaspoon Mexican chilli powder

2 tablespoons finely ground freshly cracked black pepper

2 tablespoons finely ground kosher salt

Sauce

250 ml (9 fl oz) tomato sauce (ketchup)

100 ml (3½ fl oz) water

2 tablespoons apple cider vinegar

4 tablespoons brown sugar

3 tablespoons honey

1 teaspoon onion powder

1 teaspoon mustard powder

1 teaspoon finely ground freshly cracked black pepper

1 teaspoon finely ground kosher salt

Method

Remove the membrane from the underside of the ribs and trim the rib meat to ensure the thickness of the meat on top of the rib bones is consistent end to end, removing any fat chunks to reveal the rib meat only.

Make sure the rub mix is very finely ground.

Precisely apply an even layer of dry rub to the top side of the ribs and coat the back and sides, using ⅔ of the rib rub mixture.

Allow the rubbed ribs to stand for 30 minutes to soak up the rub. Re-apply a second coating of the rib rub with the remaining rub.

Heat all of the sauce ingredients in a small pot and allow to simmer for 30 minutes, then remove and cover with foil to rest.

Indirect smoke on a barbecue smoker using peach wood chips or chunks for 1 hour at 130°C (250°F).

Remove the ribs from the smoker and apply an even coating of brown sugar, avoiding lumps of sugar. Finely slice the butter and evenly apply to cover the top of the ribs. Tightly double-wrap in foil and return to the smoker with the rib meat facing down for a further 1½ hours at 130°C (250°F). Remove the ribs from smoker and rest for 30 minutes.

Unwrap the ribs, placing meat side down on a cutting surface. Carefully slice the ribs into even single ribs and turn over. Reheat the sauce and drain into a large mixing bowl. Dip each rib into a bowl of finishing sauce to evenly glaze.

Tip Select ribs that have a minimum of 2–2.5cm (¾–1 inch) of meat on top of the bone and ribs that are consistent in shape from one end of the rack to the other.

Ensure temperature of the barbecue smoker remains consistent during the cook process.

When wrapping ribs in foil, be very careful not to puncture the foil and wrap tightly to ensure no steam or liquid escapes. Taste test ribs and apply a flavor enhancer just before serving to taste.

PISTACHIO CRUSTED STICKY PORK RIBS

Prep Time: 15 minutes	Cook Time: 3 hours	Serves 4	Cooker: Barbecue Smoker	Skill Level: Medium

Method

Combine all of the rub ingredients in a bowl.

Remove the membrane from the underside of the pork ribs and apply a liberal coating of rub to completely cover all sides of the ribs.

Indirectly hot smoke the ribs for 1 hour inside a barbecue smoker at 130°C (250°F).

Remove the ribs from the smoker and drizzle with the honey, brown sugar and butter. Double wrap each rack of ribs in foil and return to the smoker for a further 1½ hours at 130°C (250°F).

Remove the ribs from the smoker, unwrap and sprinkle the crushed pistachio nuts over rib racks. Slice the ribs to serve. Serve with fresh apple slaw.

To make the apple slaw, finely slice the apples, cabbage, onion and carrots and mix with the mayonnaise, sugar, apple cider vinegar and chill until ready to serve.

Tip Experiment with different flavored smoking chips or wood chunks such as apple wood or peach wood or try wood-infused charcoal briquettes to your preferred flavor profile.

Ingredients

2 racks pork ribs

100 ml (3½ fl oz) honey

2 tablespoons brown sugar

100 g (3½ oz) unsalted butter

250 g (9 oz) crushed pistachio nuts

Rub

2 tablespoons brown sugar

1 tablespoon smoked paprika

1 teaspoon celery powder

1 teaspoon garlic powder

1 teaspoon onion powder

1 tablespoon freshly cracked black pepper, finely ground

1 tablespoon kosher salt

Slaw

2 green apples

½ white cabbage

1 red onion

2 carrots

2 tablespoons mayonnaise

1 teaspoon white sugar

¼ cup apple cider vinegar

PINEAPPLE-GLAZED SMOKED PORK RIBS

Prep Time: 10 minutes	Cook Time: 2 hours 40 minutes	Serves 4	Cooker: Barbecue Smoker & Grill Pan	Skill Level: Medium

Ingredients

2 racks pork ribs

100 g (3½ oz) butter

1 cup pineapple nectar

½ cup pineapple chunks

Rub

1 tablespoon mild Mexican chilli powder

2 tablespoons brown sugar

1 tablespoon freshly cracked black pepper, finely ground

1 tablespoon kosher salt

Method

Combine all of the rub ingredients in a bowl.

Remove the membrane from the underside of the pork ribs and apply a liberal coating of the rub to completely cover all sides of the ribs.

Indirectly hot smoke the ribs for 1 hour inside a barbecue smoker at 130°C (250°F) with apple or peach wood chunks or chips.

Remove the ribs from the smoker and drizzle half of the pineapple nectar over the ribs. Double wrap each rack of ribs in foil and butter and return to the smoker for a further 1 hour at 130°C (250°F).

Unwrap the ribs and return to the smoker. Using a glazing brush, lightly glaze the ribs with the pineapple nectar twice, 10 minutes apart.

Using high heat, grill the pineapple chunks and add to any remaining glazing sauce. Pour over sliced ribs to serve.

. . . .

Tip Add a dash of nutmeg or cinnamon to the pineapple glaze for more kick.

CRACKLING MOROCCAN PORK BELLY RIBS WITH SAFFRON RICE

Prep Time: 25 minutes	Cook Time: 3 hours minutes	Serves 4	Cooker: Barbecue Smoker, Grill Pan & Oven	Skill Level: Ace

Method

Combine all of the rub ingredients in a bowl.

Carefully remove the skin from the pork belly and set aside.

Remove the membrane from the underside of the pork ribs and the excess fat from the top of belly to leave around 2–2.5 cm (¾–1 in) of belly meat on top of the pork ribs. Coat all sides of the belly ribs with the Moroccan rub and rest for 30 minutes.

Place the belly ribs into a barbecue smoker and hot smoke over apple or peach wood for 1½ hours.

Remove from the smoker and double wrap in foil with butter and brown sugar, then return to the smoker for a further 2 hours. Rest the ribs in foil for 30 minutes before slicing and serving.

To make the crackling, pat the belly skin dry with paper towel until completely dry. Score the belly with a sharp knife into small diamond shapes. Rub the top side of the belly skin with olive oil and liberally coat the belly skin with ground kosher salt. Place in the oven on a wire rack atop a baking tray (to catch the drippings). Roast on 220°C (420°F) for 30 minutes or until bubbles start to form on top of the skin, then roast for a further 20–30 minutes on 180°C (350°F) or until all the skin has crackled. Remove from the oven and allow to cool on a rack. Slice along scores to serve as a garnish on top of the pork belly ribs.

To make the saffron rice, add the garlic to a frying pan with the butter and lightly brown. Add the rice and stir to coat the rice with the garlic butter. Add the saffron stalks and stir until mixed through. Slowly add the chicken stock to the rice to cook until the liquid is absorbed and rice is *al dente*, stirring often. Mix through the red and habanero chilli, lime zest and juice before serving.

Ingredients

1 large rack of belly on, bone in pork ribs (minimum 8 ribs)
1 tablespoon olive oil
2 tablespoons kosher salt
50 g (1¾ oz) unsalted butter
2 tablespoons brown sugar

Saffron Rice

1 garlic clove, finely chopped
50 g (1¾ oz) unsalted butter
1½ cups white rice
¼ teaspoons saffron stalks
375 ml (13 fl oz) chicken stock
1 red chilli, finely chopped
1 habanero chilli, finely chopped
zest and juice of ½ lime

Rub

1 tablespoon smoked paprika
1 teaspoon celery powder
1 teaspoon garlic powder
1 teaspoon onion powder
½ teaspoon cayenne
½ teaspoon cinnamon powder
½ teaspoon ginger powder
½ teaspoon coriander (cilantro) powder
2 tablespoons brown sugar
1 tablespoon freshly cracked black pepper, finely ground
1 tablespoon kosher salt

APRICOT & SPRING ONION PORK RIB SOUP

Prep Time: 10 minutes	Cook Time: 60 minutes	Serves 4	Cooker: Grill Pan & Pressure Cooker	Skill Level: Easy

Method

Remove the membrane from the underside of the pork ribs and season lightly with salt and pepper. Brown in a frying pan.

Melt the butter and mix with the flour.

Add all of the ingredients, except the bean sprouts, chilli and coriander, to a pressure cooker and stir well to combine. Add the pork ribs and cook for 45 minutes.

Remove the pork ribs from the soup and coarsely pull the pork rib meat from the bones, discarding the bones. Return the pulled pork to the soup and allow to stand for 15-20 minutes before serving.

Serve with bean sprouts, finely sliced red chilli and coriander to garnish.

Tip Add a splash of hot sauce to your individual bowl add some extra kick. Grill some garlic bread on the side for dunking.

Ingredients

2 racks pork ribs

1 tablespoon kosher salt

1 teaspoon finely ground freshly cracked black pepper

100 g (3½ oz) unsalted butter

2 tablespoons plain (all-purpose) flour

3 spring onions (scallions), finely chopped

375 ml (13 fl oz) apricot nectar

200 ml (7 fl oz) beef stock

1 teaspoon garlic powder

1 teaspoon onion powder

1 teaspoon celery powder

2 tablespoons hot sauce

1 cup bean sprouts, trimmed

1 red chilli

¼ bunch coriander (cilantro)

LAMB RIBS

Lamb ribs are just ethereal when cooked right. They have a heavier texture and a more pronounced natural flavor than pork or chicken ribs, making them a great lighter meal option to the beef ribs.

A key element to selecting the right lamb ribs is in the size of the lamb to start with. Generally, the younger the lamb the smaller or thinner the lamb ribs. I go for a lamb rib with at least 1–2 cm (½–¾ in) of meat on top of the bone to make cooking these worthwhile. Any thinner and you're off to a bad start.

Once you've selected your lamb rack, I find the best way to prepare these for any cooking method is to first remove the fat or skin cap on top of the racks.

Removing the fat cap allows much better flavor and or smoke penetration and a very even cook.

I don't find it necessary to remove the membrane from the underside of the lamb ribs if I am cutting them into singles, but you certainly can do so if you wish.

If slicing the lamb ribs into singles, the membrane is a key factor in holding the lamb meat to the bone so it doesn't slide right off.

With whole racks of lamb ribs, I'll usually take the membrane off as I'm most likely going to serve them with other sides in a meal rather than a finger-food type of snack. Removing the membrane allows your guests to easily cut the racks on their plate.

GRILLED LAMB RIB SAN CHOY BOW

Prep Time: 30 minutes	Cook Time: 1 hour	Serves 4	Cooker: Barbecue Grill & Grill Pan	Skill Level: Ace

Method

Trim off any excess fat from the rib racks and trim into individual ribs.

In a large bowl, combine all the marinade ingredients. Liberally coat each individual rib with the marinade and place the marinated ribs into a sealable bag. Pour into the bag any leftover marinade, seal and chill in the fridge overnight or if in a hurry, at least 1 hour.

Crack the eggs and combine with the buttermilk. Add 1 teaspoon freshly cracked black pepper and 1 teaspoon kosher salt and stir lightly.

Add 2 tablespoons olive oil to a grill pan and pour in egg mixture. Scramble the eggs over medium heat until all liquid has evaporated and the egg is fluffy. Once the egg is cooked, remove from the pan and chop into small pieces and set aside.

Chop the button mushrooms and water chestnuts into small cubes and shallow-fry in a grill pan with 50 g (1¾ oz) butter and 1 garlic clove.

Light the charcoal and prepare the heat to approximately 150°C (300°F).

Cover the corn cobs with the corn rub and grill over direct heat with the lamb ribs.

Grill the lamb ribs over direct heat on all sides until lightly charred and remove from the grill. Slice the meat off the bones and dice into small pieces and set aside.

Slice the grilled corn kernels off the cob and set aside.

In a large mixing bowl combine the shallots, fried mushrooms, water chestnuts, red chilli, cashews, scrambled egg, grilled corn kernels and chopped lamb.

Spoon the combined mixture into the cos lettuce leaves and garnish with fried noodles.

Ingredients

3 racks of lamb ribs (approximately 6 bones per rack)
4 large eggs
50 ml (1¾ fl oz) buttermilk
1 teaspoon kosher salt
1 tablespoon freshly cracked black pepper
2 tablespoons olive oil
1 cup button mushrooms
1 small tin of water chestnuts
50 g (1¾ oz) unsalted butter
1 garlic clove
2 corn cobs
½ cup finely chopped shallots
½ red chilli
½ cup cashews, crushed
8 cos (romaine) lettuce leaves
1 cup fried noodles

Corn Rub

1 tablespoon freshly cracked black pepper
1 teaspoon celery salt
1 teaspoon agave sugar
1 teaspoon kosher salt

Marinade

50 ml (1¾ fl oz) sesame oil
50 ml (1¾ fl oz) peanut oil
2 tablespoons hoisin sauce
1 tablespoon soy sauce
3 garlic cloves
1 piece of ginger (approximately 2 cm x 3 cm/¾ in x 1¼ in)
1 tablespoon hot sauce
½ red chilli

SMOKED LAMB RIBS WITH TORTILLA ESPANOLA

Prep Time: 45 minutes	Cook Time: 3 hour 30 minutes	Serves 4	Cooker: Barbecue Smoker, Grill Pan & Pot	Skill Level: Ace

Method

Ribs

Trim excess fat from ribs and ensure that the ribs which have minimal to no meat on them are trimmed off and discarded. Liberally coat the remaining full racks of lamb ribs with the rub and add to the smoker using the indirect cooking method. Use applewood infused charcoal briquettes, or original flavour briquettes with apple wood chunks.

Cook ribs on smoker for 1.5 hours at 105°C (225°F) and remove and double wrap in foil with 1 tablespoon brown sugar and 50 g (1¾ oz) butter per rack. Return to the smoker for a further 1.5 hours at 105°C (225°F) and then remove to rest in the foil for at least 15 minutes.

Tortilla Espanola

Peel and grate potatoes and place into a large mixing bowl, then season potatoes with salt, pepper, smoked paprika and add in finely chopped garlic and onions, red and jalapeno peppers.

Heat 50 ml (1¾ fl oz) olive oil in large pan, add potato mix and lightly fry until golden and remove from pan and drain oil. Add 8 whisked eggs to potato mix and combine.

Heat 50 ml (1¾ fl oz) olive oil in large pan and reduce to medium/low heat. Add mixture and fry on low heat until crisp and golden on bottom.

Carefully remove mixture once bottom is crisp and golden, add 50 ml (1¾ fl oz) more oil to pan and cook second side of mixture. Remove from pan, allow to cool slightly before serving.

Carrots

In a medium size pot, add peeled carrots cut into 1 cm (½ in) thick slices to 400 ml (13½ fl oz) of water or enough to just cover the carrots. Add two tablespoons of honey and one tablespoon of brown sugar and stir to combine. Bring to the boil and then turn down to simmer for 30 minutes or until carrots soften and honey water reduces to a saucy texture. Allow carrots to rest in honey water until ready to serve. Garnish carrots with a pinch of kosher salt when on the plate.

Ingredients

3 racks of lamb ribs (approx. 6 bones per rack or more)
4 large carrots
50 g (1¾ oz) honey
1 tbsp kosher salt

Rub

2 tbsp fresh cracked pepper
2 tbsp kosher salt
2 tbsp brown sugar
1 tsp celery powder
1 tsp onion powder
1 tsp garlic powder
1 tsp smoked paprika
1 tsp coriander powder

Tortilla Espanola

6 large washed potatoes
1 large red onion
8 large eggs
150 ml (5 fl oz) extra virgin olive oil
1 large jalapeno pepper
1 large red pepper
1 tbsp smoked paprika
1 tbsp agave sugar
2 cloves garlic
1 tsp cracked pepper
1 tsp kosher salt

MINT, ROSEMARY & SMOKED HONEY LAMB RIBS

Prep Time: 45 minutes	Cook Time: 2 hours 10 minutes	Serves 4	Cooker: Barbecue Smoker	Skill Level: Medium

Method

Combine the rub ingredients in a bowl.

Trim off any excess fat from the rib racks and leave the racks whole. Lightly coat each full rib rack with peanut oil and then apply a liberal coating of the rub to all sides of the ribs. Allow the rub to soak into the ribs for 30 minutes before grilling.

Light the charcoal and prepare the heat to approximately 130°C (250°F). Use apple or peach wood for smoking.

Smoke the lamb ribs for 90 minutes, then remove from the smoker. Double wrap in foil with the butter and brown sugar, then return to the smoker for a further 90 minutes.

Allow the ribs to rest in foil and slice into individual ribs before serving. Serve with a drizzle of smoked honey and finely chopped mint.

Ingredients

3 racks of lamb ribs (approximately 6 ribs per rack)
50 ml (1¾ fl oz) peanut oil
150 g (5½ oz) unsalted butter
100 g (3½ oz) brown sugar
100 ml (3½ fl oz) smoked honey
1 small bunch mint leaves for garnish

Rub

1 tablespoon agave sugar
1 tablespoon brown sugar
1 teaspoon onion powder
1 teaspoon garlic powder
1 teaspoon smoked paprika
2 tablespoons freshly cracked black pepper
2 tablespoons kosher salt

Tip Serve as a snack on footy night or with a spicy apple slaw as a light lunch. Substitute mint with coriander for a different flavor profile.

MEDITERRANEAN LAMB RIBS

Prep Time: 30 minutes	Cook Time: 45 minutes	Serves 4	Cooker: Barbecue Grill & Cook Pot	Skill Level: Medium

Method

Combine the rub ingredients in a bowl.

Trim off any excess fat from the rib racks and trim into individual ribs. Lightly coat each rib with peanut oil and then apply a liberal coating of the rub to all sides of the ribs.

Light the charcoals and prepare the heat to approximately 150°C (300°F).

In a pot, add the chicken stock, water and couscous and bring to the boil. Reduce the heat to allow the couscous to simmer. Add the agave sugar and a pinch of saffron, stirring occasionally.

Remove from the heat once the couscous is *al dente* and allow to cool slightly before draining any excess liquid.

In a large bowl, combine the drained couscous with the chopped dates and chilli. Squeeze the lime juice over the mixture and add the orange zest. Mix to combine

Grill the lamb ribs directly over the coals until slightly charred and remove to rest for 5 minutes before serving.

Serve with the couscous and a dollop of Greek yoghurt on the side with cashew nuts and coriander to garnish.

Ingredients

4 racks lamb ribs (approximately 6 bones per rack)
50 ml (1¾ fl oz) peanut oil
375 ml (13 fl oz) chicken stock
250 ml (9 fl oz) water
2 cups couscous
1 tablespoon agave sugar
1 pinch saffron stalks
½ cup pitted dates, finely chopped
1 red chilli, finely chopped
juice of 1 lime
zest of ½ orange
Greek yoghurt, to serve
½ cup cashew nuts to garnish
½ bunch coriander (cilantro) to garnish

Rub

1 tablespoon coriander (cilantro) powder
1 tablespoon cumin
1 tablespoon brown sugar
1½ tablespoons kosher salt
1 teaspoon medium chilli powder
1 teaspoon cinnamon powder
1 teaspoon freshly cracked black pepper
1 teaspoon allspice
1 teaspoon garlic powder
1 teaspoon onion powder

DRY-FRIED LAMB RIBS

░░

Prep Time: 45 minutes	Cook Time: 15 minutes	Serves 6	Cooker: Deep-fryer	Skill Level: Easy

Method

Remove the excess fat from the lamb rib racks. Slice the ribs into individual pieces and lightly coat with peanut oil.

Combine all the rub ingredients in a mixing bowl and coat all the sides of the lamb ribs. Set aside any excess rub.

Chill the rubbed lamb ribs in the fridge for 30 minutes and then re-coat with the excess rub.

Preheat a deep-fryer to 180°C (350°F) and fry the lamb ribs in small batches for 3 minutes per batch and set aside.

In a small bowl, add the Greek yoghurt, hot sauce and finely chopped spring onions, coriander and mint. Serve as a dipping sauce with the fried lamb ribs.

· ·

Tip Add more chilli to the rub and hot sauce to the dip to spice it up. Change up the rub ingredients to suit your preference.

Ingredients
4 racks lamb ribs (approximately 6 ribs per rack)
50 ml (1¾ fl oz) peanut oil

Rub
6 tablespoons freshly cracked black pepper
4 tablespoons kosher salt
2 tablespoons rosemary powder
2 teaspoons garlic powder
2 teaspoons onion powder
2 teaspoons celery powder
2 teaspoons chilli powder

Sauce
300 ml (10½ fl oz) Greek yoghurt
1 teaspoon hot sauce
¼ cup chopped spring onions (scallions)
¼ coriander (cilantro)
¼ mint

CRUMBED ROSEMARY & MINT LAMB RIBS

Prep Time: 30 minutes	Cook Time: 45 minutes	Serves 6	Cooker: Deep-fryer	Skill Level: Easy

Method

Remove the excess fat from the lamb rib racks. Slice the ribs into individual pieces and lightly coat each rib with peanut oil. Apply a liberal coating of the rub to each lamb rib and chill the ribs in the fridge for 30 minutes.

Place the plain flour in a bowl, and the eggs and buttermilk in a second bowl and the panko breadcrumbs in a third bowl.

Once the lamb ribs have chilled, rub each rib in the flour, then the egg/milk mixture and then the breadcrumbs and set aside until all coated.

Preheat a deep-fryer to 180°C (350°F) and deep-fry the lamb ribs in small batches (depending on the size of the fryer) for 3–4 minutes per batch, ensuring a golden colored crumb coating.

In a small bowl, combine the Japanese mayonnaise, hot sauce and mint leaves and serve as a dipping sauce with crumbed lamb ribs.

Ingredients

4 racks of lamb ribs (approximately 6 bones per rack)
100 ml (3½ fl oz) peanut oil

Rub

3 tablespoons freshly cracked black pepper
2 tablespoons kosher salt
1 tablespoon rosemary powder
1 teaspoon garlic powder
1 teaspoon onion powder
1 teaspoon celery powder

Crumbs

300 g (10½ oz) plain (all-purpose) flour
4 eggs
50 ml (1¾ fl oz) buttermilk
500 g (1 lb 2 oz) panko breadcrumbs

Sauce

250 ml (9 fl oz) Japanese mayonnaise
1 tablespoon hot sauce
¼ cup finely chopped mint leaves

Tip Substitute mint with coriander for a different flavor profile.

CHAR SIU LAMB RIBS

Prep Time: 15 minutes (plus overnight marinade)	Cook Time: 30 minutes	Serves 4	Cooker: Barbecue Grill & Cook Pot	Skill Level: Medium

Method

Trim off any excess fat from the rib racks.

In a large bowl, combine all the marinade ingredients. Liberally coat the rib racks with the marinade and place the marinated ribs into a sealable bag. Pour into the bag any leftover marinade, seal and chill in fridge overnight or if in a hurry, at least 1 hour.

Light the charcoals and prepare the heat to approximately 150°C (300°F).

Add the rice to a pot with water and kosher salt and bring to the boil. Allow to simmer and stir the rice occasionally. Remove the rice once it becomes fluffy and just past *al dente*, then drain. Run the rice through a colander with cold water to cool the rice and remove any excess starch.

In a large mixing bowl, add the cooled rice and stir in the raw sugar and rice wine vinegar. Set aside.

Place the marinated ribs on the grill over direct heat and grill on all sides until slightly charred. Remove and allow to cool slightly before slicing and serving.

Serve with the sushi rice garnished with cashews, red chilli and coriander.

Ingredients

3 racks lamb ribs (approximately 6 bones per rack)
315 g (11 oz/1½ cups) sushi rice
500 ml (17 fl oz) water
1 teaspoon kosher salt
2 tablespoons raw sugar
1 tablespoon rice wine vinegar
40 g (1½ oz) cashew nuts, crushed
1 red chilli, finely chopped
1 bunch coriander (cilantro), finely chopped

Marinade

2 tablespoons honey
1 tablespoon hoisin sauce
1 tablespoon sweet soy sauce
2 tablespoons rice wine vinegar
1 teaspoon red food coloring
1 tablespoon Chinese five-spice powder

Tip If you want to make sushi, trim the lamb off the bones and combine with the sushi rice, Japanese mayonnaise and seaweed paper to make nori rolls.

BUTTERSCOTCH LAMB RIBS

Prep Time: 20 minutes	Cook Time: 2 hours 30 minutes	Serves 4	Cooker: Grill Pan, Cook Pots & Barbecue S`moker	Skill Level: Medium

Method

Combine the rub ingredients in a bowl.

Trim off any excess fat from the rib racks and lightly coat each rib rack with peanut oil, then apply a liberal coating of the rub to all sides of the ribs.

Light the charcoals and prepare the heat to approximately 130°C (250°F).

Smoke the rib racks for 60 minutes using apple or peach wood for the smoke. Remove the ribs from the barbecue smoker. Double wrap the ribs with foil with 50 g (1¾ oz) butter per rack. Cook at 130°C (250°F) for a further 60 minutes, then remove to rest for 10 minutes before serving.

In a large pot, add the chopped potatoes and enough water to just cover the potatoes. Add the kosher salt and bring to the boil. Allow to simmer for approximately 30 minutes. Remove the potatoes from the heat when they are very soft and drain.

Using the potato pot, sprinkle with the potato mash rub and 100 g (3½ oz) of the butter and thoroughly combine until creamy. Add a dash of full cream milk if desired to thin the mixture, or alternatively more butter to desired consistency. Once smooth and creamy, stir in onion powder, celery powder, kosher salt and fresh cracked black pepper.

In a separate small pot, combine the brown sugar and butter and stir over high heat until smooth and golden, slowly add cream until desired thickness, then set aside.

In a grill pan, shallow-fry the asparagus in olive oil until just charred, adding a pinch of salt during the process to coat the asparagus.

Serve individually sliced lamb ribs on top of the potato mash, with grilled asparagus on the side. Drizzle with butterscotch sauce to garnish.

Ingredients

3 racks of lamb ribs (approximately 6 bones per rack)
50 ml (1¾ fl oz) peanut oil
150 g (5½ oz) unsalted butter
2 bunches asparagus (or 12 pieces)
50 ml (1¾ fl oz) olive oil
1 teaspoon kosher salt

Rub

2 tablespoons brown sugar
2 tablespoons freshly cracked black pepper
2 tablespoons kosher salt
1 teaspoon smoked paprika
1 teaspoon onion powder
1 teaspoon garlic powder

Potato Mash

6 large potatoes, cut into 4 cm (1½ in) cubes
1 liter (35 fl oz) water
½ teaspoon kosher salt
100 g (3½ oz) unsalted butter
50 ml (1¾ fl oz) full cream milk
½ teaspoon onion powder
½ teaspoon celery powder
½ teaspoon freshly cracked black pepper

Butterscotch Sauce

125 g (4½ oz) brown sugar
½ cup thickened cream
125 g (4½ oz) unsalted butter

BEEF RIBS

There's nothing more primitive than chowing down on a foot-long beef rib straight off the fire. If that method isn't overly appealing, not to worry, I've come up with some more refined ways of preparing some tasty beef ribs to suit any meal setting.

Beef short ribs can be incredibly succulent and tender and are simple to cook.

I like to have my butcher prepare me some racks of 3 to 5 bones per rack and around 20 cm (8 in) long which gives me just enough meat per bone to make a single or half portion per person (depending on who you're feeding).

Preparing beef ribs is pretty simple and very similar to preparing the pork or lamb ribs. You definitely want to take the fat cap and silver skin off the top of the meat to reveal a single layer of pure meaty goodness that can soak up the rub, seasoning and/or smoke depending on how it's cooked.

Boneless beef short rib meat can be easier to work with in some recipes or cooking methods and you'll usually find that your butcher has already taken the fat and silver skin off for you. Chances are, you're also paying a bit less because of the lack of bone weight on the scales.

Beef back ribs are usually a lot thinner in meat than the short ribs but can be just as tasty. I'll usually take the membrane off from the underside of the back ribs so I can get as much flavor into the meat that is in between the bones.

Taking the membrane off the bottom of the ribs will most likely result in the bone falling off during or at the end of the cooking process and is something to keep in mind depending on how you want to serve or present the ribs.

Another way you can ensure smoke and flavor penetration into the underside of the beef ribs is to score the membrane in a criss-cross fashion without totally detaching the membrane from the rib itself.

I select a beef rib rack that has plenty of visible marbling which I know will enhance the flavor and texture, particularly with the hot smoking method.

Finding a more marbled beef rib will assist greatly with the low 'n' slow barbecuing as the marble (fat) will render down during the process into a juicy liquid and ensure that the center of the meat stays very moist.

For thrillseekers, you can catch the dripping fat from the beef ribs and use in your grill pan for a flavorful frying oil.

SMOKED BEEF RIB SURF 'N' TURF

Prep Time: 20 minutes	Cook Time: 6 hours 30 minutes	Serves 4	Cooker: Barbecue Smoker & Grill Pan	Skill Level: Medium

Method

Preheat a barbecue smoker to 140°C (275°F).

Remove the silver skin from the top of the short ribs and remove the membrane from the underside of the beef ribs. Massage the oil onto all sides of the ribs to apply a light coating.

Combine the rub mixture in a small bowl or container and then evenly apply to the oiled ribs. Depending on the size of the ribs, more mixture may be required. Ensure all the rib meat is covered with the rub, concentrating on the top and sides of the meat and then the underside.

Place the ribs bone down in the barbecue smoker and add hickory wood chips or chunks in small batches in the first 2 hours, being careful to ensure a constant but light and even smoke.

Allow the ribs to cook for a further 1 hour (3 hours total), then remove from the smoker and double-wrap with foil and butter.

Cook in the foil for a further 3 hours.

Remove the head and innards from the bugs and slice the bug in half, lengthways. Season the bug with kosher salt and pepper and shallow-fry meat side down in a grill pan with the finely diced garlic and 100 g (3½ oz) of unsalted butter. Once cooked, remove the meat from the shell and keep the butter for a finishing sauce.

Peel, cube and boil the sweet potatoes until soft. Drain the water, add half of the butter and season with salt and pepper and stir well. Continue to add the butter until the potato mash is creamy, thin and slightly runny. Add a dash of cream or milk if required to thin the mash.

Remove the beef ribs from the barbecue and carefully open the foil to expel some steam to prevent further cooking. Lightly close the foil back over the ribs and rest for 20 minutes before slicing and serving.

Serve the beef ribs sliced off the bone, topped with the bugs tails, garlic butter finishing sauce and coriander and lime zest, to garnish.

Ingredients

2 racks beef short ribs (4 bones per rack)
2 tablespoons peanut oil (or olive oil)
100 g (3½ oz) unsalted butter
4 bugs, sliced in half lengthways to provide 8 halves
2 tablespoons freshly cracked black pepper
2 tablespoons kosher salt
1 garlic clove, finely diced
100 g (3½ oz) of unsalted butter
¼ bunch coriander (cilantro), chopped
zest of 1 lime

Rub

2 tablespoons freshly cracked black pepper
2 tablespoons kosher salt
2 tablespoons brown sugar
1 tablespoon onion powder
1 tablespoon garlic powder
1 tablespoon smoked paprika

Creamy Mash

2 large sweet potatoes
125 g (4½ oz) unsalted butter
1 tablespoon kosher salt
1 teaspoon freshly cracked black pepper

MASSAMAN BEEF RIBS

Prep Time: 15 minutes	Cook Time: 60 minutes	Serves 2	Cooker: Grill Pan & Pressure Cooker	Skill Level: Easy

Ingredients

4 beef short ribs (approximately 1 kg/2 lb 4 oz)
2 tablespoons freshly cracked black pepper
2 tablespoons kosher salt
375 ml (13 fl oz) coconut cream
1 brown onion, diced
2 bay leaves
2 tablespoons sugar
¾ red chilli
2 tablespoons massaman curry paste
2 carrots, roughly chopped into chunks
1 large sweet potato, diced
200 g (7 oz) jasmine rice
¼ cup cashews, crushed
½ cup bean sprouts
1 red chilli, finely sliced
2 tablespoons dried shallots

Method

Remove any excess fat from the beef short ribs and rub liberally with salt and cracked pepper. Set aside the leftover salt and pepper. Add the oil to the grill pan over medium heat and brown the beef short ribs.

Place the browned beef ribs in a pressure cooker along with the coconut cream, diced brown onion, bay leaves, sugar, ¾ red chilli and curry paste and cook for 30 minutes.

Add the carrots and sweet potato to the pressure cooker. Remove the bay leaves and cook for a further 25 minutes.

Remove the beef ribs from the pressure cooker and discard the rib membrane and bones. Chop the beef into large chunks and return to the mixture, stirring to combine.

Boil the jasmine rice in a pan until *al dente*.

Serve with a garnish of crushed cashew nuts, bean sprouts, finely sliced red chilli and dried shallots to taste.

. . . .

Tip Deep fry a handful of papadums to scoop up some of the tasty broth.

HOT 'N' SPICY SMOKED BEEF BACK RIBS

Prep Time: 10 minutes	Cook Time: 6 hours 30 minutes	Serves 4	Cooker: Barbecue Smoker	Skill Level: Medium

Ingredients

2 racks beef short ribs (4–5 bones per rack)

2 tablespoons peanut oil (or olive oil)

100 g (3½ oz) unsalted butter

1 small red chilli, finely sliced

¼ bunch coriander (cilantro), chopped

Rub

2 tablespoons freshly cracked black pepper

2 tablespoons kosher salt

1 tablespoon brown sugar

1 tablespoon onion powder

1 tablespoon garlic powder

1 tablespoon smoked paprika

1 tablespoon chilli powder

Sauce

1 large chipotle pepper

1 teaspoon agave sugar

zest of 1 lime

200 g (7 oz) light sour cream

Method

Preheat the barbecue smoker to 140°C (275°F).

Remove the silver skin from the top of the short ribs and remove the membrane from under side of the beef ribs. Massage the oil onto all sides of the ribs to apply a light coating.

Combine the rub mixture in a small bowl or container, then evenly apply to oiled ribs. Depending on the size of the ribs, more mixture may be required. Ensure all areas of the rib meat is covered with rub, concentrating on the top and sides of the meat and the underside.

Place the ribs bone down in the barbecue smoker and add hickory wood chips or chunks in small batches in the first 1½ hours, being careful to ensure a constant but light and even smoke.

Remove the ribs from the smoker. Double-wrap with butter and return to the smoker to cook for a further 2 hours.

Add the chipotle, sour cream, pepper, agave sugar and the lime zest to a bowl and blend using an electric mixer until combined. Store in the fridge until ready to serve.

Remove the beef ribs from the barbecue and carefully open the foil to expel some steam to prevent further cooking. Lightly close the foil back over the ribs and rest for 20 minutes before slicing and serving.

Serve the ribs sliced off the bone with a drizzle of chipotle cream, coriander and red chilli to garnish.

Tip Serve with sides including mac and cheese, grilled corn or cornbread in winter, or with a side salad or spicy coleslaw in summer.

The ribs can be served sliced off the bone or caveman style on the bone.

HONEY BBQ SMOKED BEEF SHORT RIBS

Prep Time: 10 minutes	Cook Time: 5 hours	Serves 4	Cooker: Barbecue Smoker	Skill Level: Medium

Method

Preheat a barbecue smoker to 140°C (275°F).

Remove any silver skin from the short ribs and massage oil onto all sides of the ribs to apply a light coating.

Combine the rub mixture in a small bowl or container, then evenly apply to the oiled ribs. Depending on the size of the ribs, more mixture may be required. Ensure all areas of the rib meat is covered with the rub.

Place the ribs in the barbecue smoker and add peach or apple wood chips or chunks in small batches in the first 2 hours, being careful to ensure a constant but light and even smoke.

Remove from the smoker and double wrap with foil and butter. Return to the smoker to cook in the foil for a further 2½ hours.

Unwrap the ribs from the foil and drizzle the honey over the ribs twice over a 30 minute period before removing and slicing to serve.

Tip Serve with sides including mac and cheese, grilled corn or cornbread in winter, or with a side salad or spicy coleslaw in summer.

Ingredients

2 x 1 kg (2 lb 4 oz) portions of boneless beef short ribs

2 tablespoons peanut oil (or olive oil)

100 g (3½ oz) unsalted butter

100 g (3½ oz) honey

Rub

2 tablespoons freshly cracked black pepper

2 tablespoons kosher salt

1 tablespoon brown sugar

1 tablespoon onion powder

1 tablespoon garlic powder

1 tablespoon sweet paprika

1 teaspoon cinnamon powder

HICKORY-SMOKED BEEF SHORT RIBS

Prep Time: 10 minutes	Cook Time: 6 hours 30 minutes	Serves 4	Cooker: Barbecue Smoker	Skill Level: Medium

Ingredients

2 racks beef short ribs (4–5 bones per rack)

2 tablespoons peanut oil (or olive oil)

100 g (3½ oz) unsalted butter

Rub

2 tablespoons freshly cracked black pepper

2 tablespoons kosher salt

2 tablespoons brown sugar

1 tablespoon onion powder

1 tablespoon garlic powder

1 tablespoon smoked paprika

Method

Preheat the barbecue smoker to 140°C (275°F).

Remove the silver skin from the top of the short ribs and also remove the membrane from underside of the beef ribs. Massage the oil onto all sides of the ribs to apply a light coating.

Combine the rub mixture in a small bowl or container, then evenly apply to the oiled ribs. Depending on the size of the ribs, more mixture may be required. Ensure all areas of the rib meat is covered with rub, concentrating on the top and sides of the meat and then the underside.

Place the ribs bone down in the barbecue smoker and add hickory wood chips or chunks in small batches in the first 2 hours, being careful to ensure a constant but light and even smoke.

Allow the ribs to cook for a further 1 hour (3 hours total), then remove from the smoker and double-wrap with foil and butter. Cook in the foil for a further 3 hours.

Remove the beef ribs from barbecue and carefully open the foil to expel some steam to prevent further cooking. Lightly close the foil back over the ribs and rest for 20 minutes before slicing and serving.

Tip Serve with sides including mac and cheese and cornbread in winter, or with a side salad or spicy coleslaw in summer.

Can be served sliced off the bone or caveman style on the bone.

COFFEE-SMOKED BBQ BEEF SHORT RIBS

Prep Time: 10 minutes	Cook Time: 6 hours 30 minutes	Serves 4	Cooker: Barbecue Smoker	Skill Level: Medium

Method

Preheat a barbecue smoker to 140°C (275°F).

Remove the silver skin from the top of the short ribs and also remove the membrane from under side of the beef ribs.
Massage the oil onto all sides of the ribs to apply a light coating.

Combine the rub mixture in a small bowl or container, then evenly apply to oiled ribs. Depending on the size of the ribs, more mixture may be required. Ensure all areas of the rib meat is covered with the rub, concentrating on the top and sides of the meat then the underside.

Place the ribs bone down in the barbecue smoker and add hickory wood chips or chunks in small batches in the first 2 hours, being careful to ensure a constant but light and even smoke.

Allow the ribs to cook for a further 1 hour (3 hours total), then remove from the smoker and double-wrap with foil and butter.

Cook in the foil for a further 3 hours.

Combine all the sauce ingredients in a pot, starting with the wet ingredients then the dry ingredients and bring to the boil.
Turn the heat down and simmer sauce in pot for a minimum of 30 minutes before removing to allow to cool.

Remove the beef ribs from the foil and baste ribs with basting brush twice over a 30 minute period, then slice to serve.

Tip Serve with sides including mac and cheese, grilled corn or cornbread in winter, or with a side salad or spicy coleslaw in summer.
Can be served sliced off the bone or caveman style on the bone.

Ingredients

2 racks beef short ribs (4–5 bones per rack)
2 tablespoons peanut oil (or olive oil)
100 g (3½ oz) unsalted butter

Rub

2 tablespoons freshly cracked black pepper
2 tablespoons kosher salt
1 tablespoon freshly ground coffee
1 tablespoon brown sugar
1 tablespoon onion powder
1 tablespoon garlic powder
1 tablespoon smoked paprika

Sauce

250 ml (9 fl oz) tomato sauce (ketchup)
100 ml (3½ fl oz) water
2 tablespoons apple cider vinegar
4 tablespoons brown sugar
3 tablespoons honey
1 teaspoon finely ground, freshly cracked black pepper
1 teaspoon finely ground kosher salt
1 teaspoon onion powder
1 teaspoon mustard powder
2 tablespoons hot sauce
1 chipotle pepper, finely diced

WARM BEEF RIB & GOAT'S CHEESE SALAD

Prep Time: 30 minutes	Cook Time: 6 hours 30 minutes	Serves 4	Cooker: Barbecue Smoker, Grill Pan & Cook Pot	Skill Level: Ace

Ingredients

2 racks beef short ribs (4–5 bones per rack)
2 tablespoons peanut oil (or olive oil)
100 g (3½ oz) unsalted butter
2 garlic cloves, finely chopped
12 large Brussels sprouts
2 tablespoons honey
2 thickly sliced bacon slices
½ loaf of ciabatta bread
1 half head of broccoli
100 ml (3½ fl oz) olive oil
100 g (3½ oz) goat's cheese
100 g (3½ oz) cashew nuts
50 g (1¾ oz) grated parmesan cheese

Rub

2 tablespoons freshly cracked black pepper
2 tablespoons kosher salt
2 tablespoons brown sugar
1 tablespoon onion powder
1 tablespoon garlic powder
1 tablespoon smoked paprika

Method

Preheat a barbecue smoker to 140°C (275°F).

Remove the silver skin from the top of the short ribs and also remove the membrane from underside of the beef ribs. Massage the oil onto all sides of the ribs to apply a light coating.

Combine the rub mixture in a small bowl or container, then evenly apply to oiled ribs. Depending on the size of the ribs, more mixture may be required. Ensure all areas of the rib meat is covered with rub, concentrating on the top and sides of the meat and then the underside.

Place the ribs bone down in the barbecue smoker and add hickory wood chips or chunks in small batches in the first 2 hours, being careful to ensure a constant but light and even smoke.

Allow the ribs to cook for a further 1 hour (3 hours total), then remove from the smoker and double-wrap with foil and butter. Cook in the foil for a further 3 hours.

Halve the Brussels sprouts, season lightly with salt and pepper and deep-fry for 3 minutes. Remove from the oil and drain on paper towel.

Slice the bacon into roughly cut chunks and lightly grill in a grill pan, then set aside.

Cube the cob loaf into 2 cm (¾ in) squared chunks and lightly grill in a grill pan with 2 finely chopped garlic cloves and butter.

Roughly chop the broccoli and add to a pot with the honey and a pinch of kosher salt.

Remove the beef ribs from the barbecue and carefully open the foil to expel some steam to prevent further cooking. Lightly close the foil back over the ribs and rest for 20 minutes before slicing and serving.

Slice the beef ribs off the bone and cube into chunks. Combine with the Brussels sprouts, bacon, bread pieces, small chunks of goat's cheese and cashew nuts.

Drizzle the olive oil to coat the finished beef and salad mix. Garnish with freshly grated parmesan cheese.

BEEF SHORT RIB POT PIE

░░

Prep Time: 15 minutes	Cook Time: 1 hour 30 minutes	Serves 2	Cooker: Grill Pan, Pressure Cooker & Oven	Skill Level: Medium

Method

Remove any excess fat from the beef short ribs and rub liberally with salt and cracked pepper. Set aside the leftover salt and pepper. Add the oil to the grill pan and brown the beef short ribs.

Place the browned beef ribs in a pressure cooker along with 100 ml (3½ fl oz) beef stock, celery powder, brown onion, garlic powder, red chilli, rough chopped tomatoes, leftover salt and pepper and pressure cook for 25 minutes.

Preheat the oven to 200°C (400°F).

Dice carrots and sweet potato into small cubes and add to the pressure cooker and cook for a further 25 minutes.

Remove the beef ribs from the pressure cooker and discard the rib membrane and bones. Chop the beef into 2–3 cm (¾–1¼ in) cubes and return to the mixture, also adding the peas. Stir to combine.

Spoon the beef rib and vegetable mixture into lightly oiled individual pie pots and cover with puff pastry. Lightly brush the puff pastry with butter and bake at 200°C (400°F) for approximately 30 minutes, or until puff pastry is crisp and golden.

Remove the pies from the oven and allow to cool before serving.

. . . .

Tip Add mushrooms and other in-season vegetables to your preference.

Add mozzarella balls to the pie for a cheesy twist.

Ingredients

4 beef short ribs (approximately 1 kg/2 lb 4 oz total)

1 tablespoon freshly cracked black pepper

1 tablespoon kosher salt

2 tablespoons olive oil

100 ml (3½ fl oz) beef stock

1 teaspoon celery powder

1 teaspoon garlic powder

1 red chilli, finely chopped

2 tomatoes, roughly chopped

2 carrots, diced

1 sweet potato, diced

½ brown onion

¼ cup green peas

50 g (1¾ oz) butter

2 sheets of puff pastry

BEEF SHORT RIB GUMBO

▨▨▨▨▨▨▨▨▨▨▨▨▨▨▨▨▨▨▨▨▨▨▨▨▨▨▨

Prep Time: 30 minutes	Cook Time: 1 hour	Serves 4	Cooker: Grill Pan & Pressure Cooker	Skill Level: Medium

Method

Remove any excess fat from the beef short ribs and rub liberally with salt and cracked pepper. Set aside leftover salt and pepper. Add oil to the grill pan and brown the beef short ribs.

Place the browned beef ribs in a pressure cooker along with the beef stock, white rice, celery powder, garlic cloves, red chilli, tomatoes, leftover salt and pepper, smoked paprika, Mexican chilli powder, white sugar, apple cider vinegar, hoisin sauce, bacon and pressure cook for 35 minutes.

Add the carrots and sweet potato to the pressure cooker and cook for a further 20 minutes.

Remove the beef ribs from the pressure cooker and discard the rib membrane and bones. Chop the beef into 2–3 cm (¾–1¼ in) cubes and return to the mixture, stirring to combine.

In a separate pan, lightly fry the squid in olive oil.

In a separate pan, lightly fry the chorizo sausage in olive oil.

Add the squid and chorizo to the finished gumbo mix and serve with a crusty bread or damper loaf.

Garnish with coriander and red chilli, to taste.

· ·

Tip Add 1 teaspoon liquid smoke to bump up the smokey flavor.
Add a dollop of Greek yoghurt to serve to make the gumbo creamy, if preferred.

Serve with a side of garlic butter damper roll or crusty bread to soak up the juicy goodness.

Ingredients

2 racks beef short ribs (8 bones total)
2 tablespoons freshly cracked black pepper
2 tablespoons kosher salt
2 tablespoons oil for frying
375 ml (13 fl oz) beef stock
300 g (10½ oz) white rice
1 teaspoon celery powder
4 garlic cloves, finely chopped
1 red chilli, finely chopped
3 tomatoes, roughly chopped
1 teaspoon smoked paprika
1 teaspoon Mexican chilli powder
3 tablespoons white sugar
2 tablespoons apple cider vinegar
2 tablespoons hoisin sauce
3 bacon slices, roughly chopped
2 carrots, diced
2 sweet potatoes, diced
1 brown onion
1 large chorizo sausage, roughly chopped
2 large squid (calamari) tubes, roughly chopped
¼ bunch coriander (cilantro)

BRAISED BEEF SHORT RIB GOULASH

Prep Time: 15 minutes	Cook Time: 1 hour 20 minutes	Serves 4	Cooker: Pressure Cooker	Skill Level: Easy

Method

Pan-fry the beef ribs to brown the meat.

Roughly slice the bacon into small strips. Dilute the vegemite in 100 ml (3½ fl oz) of hot water to form a stock.

Place all ingredients (except bread, 2 garlic cloves, 50 ml olive oil and quail eggs) into a pressure cooker and cook for 45 minutes. Rest on warm in cooker for 30 minutes.

Finely dice remaining garlic and trim ciabatta bread into fingers. Add the garlic to the frying pan with the olive oil and shallow-fry the bread fingers until golden.

Remove the beef short ribs from the goulash and remove the bones and membrane. Chunk the beef into cubes and return to the oulash.

Lightly fry the quail eggs in the remaining garlic olive oil.

Serve in a deep bowl with the bread fingers and quail egg.

Tip Great winter dish and can be frozen and re-heated if cooking in bulk.

Add 2 tablespoons of Franks Hot Sauce or Sriracha Hot Sauce for extra kick.

Substitute vegemite with beef stock cubes if preferred.

Ingredients

4 large bone-in beef short ribs

3 bacon slices

1 tablespoon vegemite

100 ml (3½ fl oz) hot water

2 large carrots, diced

1 large sweet potato, diced

1 white onion, diced

2 anchovies

4 garlic cloves, diced

3 tomatoes, diced

1 large red chilli

2 tablespoons freshly cracked black pepper

2 tablespoons kosher salt

1 teaspoon celery powder

1 tablespoon white sugar

1 tablespoon smoked paprika

1 ciabatta bread loaf

50 ml (1¾ fl oz) olive oil

4 quail eggs

BEEF SHORT RIB PASTRAMI

░░

Prep Time: 10 minutes	Cook Time: 6 hours 30 minutes	Serves 4	Cooker: Barbecue Smoker	Skill Level: Medium

Method

Pre-heat barbecue smoker to 135°C (275°F).

Remove silver skin from the top of the short ribs and also remove the membrane from under side of the beef ribs. Massage oil onto all sides of the ribs to apply a light coating.

Combine rub mixture in a small bowl or container and then evenly apply to oiled ribs. Depending on the size of the ribs, more mixture may be required. Ensure all areas of the rib meat is covered with rub, concentrating on the top and sides of the meat and then underside.

Place ribs bone down in the barbecue smoker and add hickory wood chips or chunks in small batches in the first 2 hours being careful to ensure a constant but light and even smoke.

Allow ribs to cook for a further hour (3 hours total) and remove from smoker and double-wrap with aluminum foil and butter.

Cook in the foil for a further three hours or until the internal temperature reaches 95°C (203°F).

Remove the beef ribs from barbecue and carefully open the foil to expel some steam to prevent further cooking. Lightly close the foil back over the ribs and rest for 20 minutes before slicing and serving.

. . . .

Tip Slice thinly and add to a sandwich with pickled cabbage for a tasty lunch or serve with seasonal vegetables and a white sauce for a hearty meal.

Ingredients

2 racks beef short ribs (3–4 bones per rack)

*Beef Short Ribs to be brined for 48–72 hours prior to cooking

2 tablespoons peanut oil (or olive oil)

100 g (3½ oz) unsalted butter

1 tablespoon brown sugar

Rub

2 tablespoons fresh cracked pepper

2 tablespoons brown sugar

1 tablespoon onion powder

1 tablespoon garlic powder

1 tablespoon smoked paprika

1 teaspoon kosher salt

CHICKEN RIBS

Chicken ribs, you say? Yes, they're real and they're spectacular.

The rib cage of the chicken is often stripped for its breast meat and tenderloin, leaving no meat left on the ribs.

I've tried cutting my own chicken ribs from a whole bird many times.

My local butcher has the right chicken stripping jig and makes it look simple. I find it way easier and somewhat cheaper to buy pre-cut chicken rib singles and I buy them by the kilogram. Depending on size of the chicken and ribs, you could get as many as 30 to 40 ribs per kilogram. To note, there are only two chicken ribs of a decent size per chicken and unless you process a couple of dozen birds per week, in some ways the local butcher is the only way to go.

Because we're working with the very lean breast meat of the chicken, the chicken ribs lend themselves to hot and fast cooking or grilling for best results. Cook them too long and they'll dry out and become chewy or tough.

The chicken ribs are an excellent snack with next to no mess and great for a tasty half-time snack during the footy game. With one bone to navigate, the chicken ribs are far more easy to devour than the trusty chicken drumsticks or wings.

A word of caution though. Chicken ribs are highly, highly addictive.

SOUTHERN-STYLE CHICKEN RIBS

Prep Time: 20 minutes & overnight brine	Cook Time: 20 minutes	Serves 6	Cooker: Deep-fryer	Skill Level: Easy

Method

Place the chicken ribs and buttermilk in a sealable bag and brine overnight in the fridge. Drain the buttermilk and set the chicken ribs aside until needed.

Preheat a deep-fryer to 180°C (350°F).

In a mixing bowl, combine all the dry rub ingredients and set aside.

Combine the eggs and hot sauce in a separate mixing bowl and dip the chicken ribs in the egg mixture, then the rub mixture and set aside.

Deep-fry the chicken ribs in small batches and drain on paper towel and to cool slightly before serving with your favorite dipping sauce.

Tip Add more chilli powder to the dry rub mix for a bit more heat per bite.

Try a Japanese mayonnaise and hot sauce blended sauce.

Ingredients

24 chicken ribs

500 ml (17 fl oz) buttermilk

4 eggs

2 tablespoons hot sauce

Rub

150 g (5½ oz) plain (all-purpose) flour

1 tablespoon freshly cracked black pepper

1 tablespoons kosher salt

2 tablespoons onion powder

2 tablespoons garlic powder

2 tablespoons sweet paprika

CRUMBED CHICKEN RIBS

Prep Time: 35 minutes	Cook Time: 4 minutes	Serves 4–6	Cooker: Deep-fryer	Skill Level: Easy

Method

Apply liberal coating of rub to each chicken rib and chill ribs in fridge for 30 minutes.

Place eggs and buttermilk in a bowl and panko breadcrumbs in a second bowl.

Dip the coated ribs into the egg and buttermilk mixture and then coat well with breadcrumbs.

Pre-heat deep fryer to 180°C (350°F) and deep fry chicken ribs in small batches (depending on the size of the fryer) for 3–4 minutes per batch ensuring a golden colored crumb coating.

Place cooked ribs on paper towel to drain excess oil and serve with dipping sauces.

Tip Use this cooking method with any flavor combination in the rub to suit your preference. These are such good eating on their own but add a range of dipping sauces on the side depending on your crowd. One of my favorites is the Japanese Mayo and Hot Sauce combination.

Ingredients
24 Chicken Ribs

Rub
1 tablespoon fresh cracked black pepper
1 tablespoon kosher salt
1 tablespoon rosemary powder
1 teaspoon garlic powder
1 teaspoon onion powder
1 teaspoon celery powder

Crumbs
500 g (17½ oz) panko breadcrumbs
4 eggs
50 ml (1¾ oz) buttermilk
2 cups plain flour

SMOKED HONEY SESAME CHICKEN RIBS

Prep Time: 10 minutes	Cook Time: 25 minutes	Serves 6	Cooker: Grill Pan	Skill Level: Easy

Method

Lightly coat the chicken ribs with the peanut oil.

In a mixing bowl, combine the rub ingredients and apply a liberal coating to the chicken ribs.

In a grill pan, add the canola oil and shallow-fry the chicken ribs, turning the ribs several times until cooked through. Cook in small batches and place the ribs on paper towel to drain.

Place all the cooked chicken ribs into a large mixing bowl and drizzle with the smoked honey and mix until all lightly coated. Sprinkle the sesame seeds on the honey-coated ribs and serve.

Tip Garnish with chopped coriander for a fresh kick. Serve on a bed of fluffy white rice garnished with crushed cashews and coriander.

Ingredients

24 chicken ribs

100 ml (3½ fl oz) peanut oil

100 ml (3½ fl oz) canola oil

100 ml (3½ fl oz) smoked honey

¼ cup sesame seeds

Rub

2 tablespoons freshly cracked black pepper

2 tablespoons kosher salt

2 tablespoons brown sugar

1 teaspoon garlic powder

1 teaspoon onion powder

1 teaspoon sweet paprika

FLAME-GRILLED SATAY CHICKEN RIBS

Prep Time: 30 minutes	Cook Time: 20 minutes	Serves 4 (with rice)	Cooker: Barbecue grill	Skill Level: Medium

Method

Combine all the marinade ingredients in large mixing bowl and mix well. Set one-third of the mixture aside to use as a dipping sauce.

Coat the chicken ribs with the remaining two-thirds of the marinade. Chill in the fridge for 30 minutes.

Prepare the barbecue for direct heat grilling.

Grill the chicken ribs over direct heat, turning regularly until lightly charred and the chicken is cooked through. This should take about 15 minutes, depending on how far away the chicken is from the direct heat.

Serve with chopped coriander and the satay marinade dipping sauce.

Tip Serve on a bed of fluffy rice and pour satay sauce over the ribs for a more fancy serving suggestion.

Ingredients

24 chicken ribs

1 bunch coriander (cilantro), chopped

Marinade

250 ml (9 fl oz) coconut cream

50 ml (1¾ oz) peanut oil

60 g (2¼ oz) crunchy peanut butter

juice of 1 lime

1 tablespoon sweet soy sauce

1 teaspoon curry powder

½ teaspoon turmeric

1 teaspoon agave sugar

½ teaspoon mild chilli powder

½ teaspoon onion powder

½ teaspoon garlic powder

CHILLI CHICKEN RIBS

Prep Time: 10 minutes	Cook Time: 40 minutes	Serves 6	Cooker: Barbecue Smoker	Skill Level: Medium

Method

Combine all the rub ingredients in a bowl and mix well. Coat all the sides of the chicken ribs and set aside.

Preheat a barbecue smoker to 140°C (275°F). Smoke the ribs over indirect heat for 20 minutes.

Combine all of the sauce ingredients in a small saucepan and bring to the boil. Stir well to combine for 1–2 minutes.

Remove the sauce from the heat and allow to cool slightly. Pour the sauce into a large mixing bowl.

Dip each chicken rib into the sauce to fully coat and baste.

Return the ribs to the smoker for a further 10 minutes. Apply another coat of basting sauce to the ribs and return to the smoker for a further 5 minutes.

Slice open one of the largest chicken ribs to ensure meat is cooked through before removing the ribs from the smoker. Serve with the dip.

Ingredients

16 chicken ribs, individually cut

Rub
2 tablespoons mild chilli powder
2 tablespoons brown sugar
1 tablespoon garlic powder
1 tablespoon onion powder
1 tablespoon agave sugar

Sauce
2 garlic cloves
250 ml (9 fl oz) medium hot sauce
1 piece of ginger (2 cm x 2 cm/¾ in x ¾ in)
1 small habanero pepper
juice of 1 lime
50 ml (1¾ fl oz) apple cider vinegar
100 g (3½ oz) butter
1 teaspoon hoisin sauce

Dip
300 ml (10½ fl oz) Japanese mayonnaise
2 tablespoons hot sauce

BUFFALO CHICKEN RIBS

Prep Time: 20 minutes	Cook Time: 40 minutes	Serves 6	Cooker: Barbecue Smoker & Pot	Skill Level: Ace

Method

Prepare a barbecue smoker for indirect smoking at 140°C (275°F).

Combine the sauce ingredients in a pot, stir well and bring to the boil. Reduce the heat and simmer for 15 minutes, then remove from the heat and allow to cool.

Combine the rub ingredients in a mixing bowl and mix thoroughly.

Lightly coat the chicken ribs in the peanut oil and then apply a liberal coating of the rub to the ribs.

In a grill pan, add 50 g (1¾ oz) of the butter and melt. Add the plain flour and stir until combined. Slowly add the milk until combined and smooth. Add the blue cheese and stir until melted, then remove from heat.

Indirect cook the ribs on the barbecue smoker using apple or peach wood for 15 minutes, or until the dry rub starts to look baked.

Dip each rib into the sauce mixture and return to the barbecue to set the sauce. Repeat the sauce process again after 10 minutes and cook for a total of approximately 35 minutes. Slice into one of the larger ribs to ensure the chicken is cooked through.

Serve the chicken ribs with blue cheese dipping sauce on the side.

Ingredients

24 chicken ribs
100 ml (3½ fl oz) peanut oil

Hot Sauce

200 ml (7 fl oz) hot sauce
100 g (3½ oz) unsalted butter
1 tablespoon apple cider vinegar
1 teaspoon Worcestershire sauce
1 teaspoon hoisin sauce
1 teaspoon sweet soy sauce
1 teaspoon freshly cracked black pepper
1 teaspoon kosher salt

Rub

2 tablespoons freshly cracked black pepper
2 tablespoons kosher salt
1 tablespoon garlic powder
1 tablespoon onion powder
1 tablespoon smoked paprika
1 tablespoon agave sugar

Blue Cheese Sauce

50 g (1¾ oz) unsalted butter
1 tablespoon plain (all-purpose) flour
200 ml (7 fl oz) full cream milk
75 g (2½ oz) blue cheese

Tip Replace the blue cheese with a vintage cheese for a more mild cheese sauce.

Add ½ teaspoon white pepper for a peppery white cheesy sauce.

BEER-BATTERED CHICKEN RIBS

Prep Time: 20 minutes	Cook Time: 30 minutes	Serves 6	Cooker: Deep-fryer	Skill Level: Medium

Method

Combine all of the rub ingredients in a large mixing bowl and mix well. Add the chicken ribs and liberally coat with the rub. Set aside.

In a separate mixing bowl, combine the cornflour, self-raising flour and plain flour and mix well. Slowly add the beer, stirring well to combine. Allow the batter to stand for 10 minutes.

Preheat a deep-fryer to 180°C (350°F).

To make the cheese sauce, melt the butter in a grill pan. Add the plain flour and stir until combined. Slowly add in the milk until combined and smooth. Add the vintage cheese and stir until melted, then remove from the heat.

Dip each rib in the batter and place directly into the hot oil. Fry in small batches. Drain the ribs on paper towel.

Serve with vintage cheese dipping sauce.

Ingredients

24 chicken ribs

Rub

2 tablespoons freshly cracked black pepper

2 tablespoons kosher salt

1 tablespoon onion powder

1 tablespoon smoked paprika

1 teaspoon garlic powder

1 teaspoon celery powder

Batter

40 g (1½ oz) cornflour (cornstarch)

40 g (1½ oz) self-raising flour

75 g (2½ oz) plain (all-purpose) flour

300 ml (10½ fl oz) dark ale

Cheese Sauce

50 g (1¾ oz) unsalted butter

1 tablespoon plain (all-purpose) flour

200 ml (7 fl oz) full cream milk

75 g (2½ oz) vintage cheese

ASIAN-STYLE CHICKEN RIBS

Prep Time: 15 minutes & marinade time	Cook Time: 30 minutes	Serves 4 people with rice	Cooker: Grill Pan	Skill Level: Easy

Ingredients

24 chicken ribs
2 tablespoons peanut oil
¼ cup chopped coriander (cilantro)
40 g (1½ oz) sesame seeds
½ cup fried shallots

Marinade

1 tablespoon peanut oil
125 ml (4 fl oz) sweet soy sauce
125 ml (4 fl oz) tomato sauce (ketchup)
1 tablespoon hoisin sauce
2 tablespoons honey
1 tablespoon hot sauce
2 garlic cloves
1 small piece of ginger
juice of 1 lime
1 tablespoon agave sugar

Method

Combine all the marinade ingredients in a large bowl. Liberally coat each individual rib with the marinade and place the marinated ribs into a sealable bag. Pour any leftover marinade into the bag, seal and chill in fridge overnight or if in a hurry, at least 1 hour.

Preheat a large grill pan and add the peanut oil.

Portion the marinated ribs into two and grill in two batches over medium heat until the chicken is cooked through (should take approximately 10 minutes per batch). Remove any charred or excess marinade from the grill pan between batches to avoid spoiling the second batch.

Place all the cooked ribs into a large mixing bowl, drizzle with the honey and garnish with chopped coriander, sesame seeds and fried shallots.

Tip Serve with a fried or sticky white rice to turn into a light meal.

TAKE TWO, LEFTOVERS

What to do with your leftover ribs?

As tasty as ribs are and as much as you would like a whole plate to yourself, the leftover meat can be even better the next day, or for a second round of cooking.

Allowing some meats to cool and refrigerate overnight or over a couple of days is going to help embed the flavors into the meat, just like a marinade.

A huge tip for prepping your leftover rib meats for their second cook up is to pull the meat from the bones whilst it is still lukewarm or hot.

Pulling the meat apart when it's cold can be a struggle and you may not get the precise portion size or texture you're after.

If you're not going to use your leftover pulled meat within a couple of days, you can vacuum seal the meat in a bag and store it for longer than usual in the fridge, or you can simply put it in a sealable (ziplock) bag and place it in the freezer.

One key element to keep in mind when re-heating your leftover meats is that the meat is already cooked and can essentially be eaten cold or as is. Ensure that you don't try and 'cook' the meat for a second time as you'll run the risk of drying it out and making it chewy, crispy or devoid of any moisture.

Carefully bring the meat back up to serving temperature and remove it from the heat.

There are a number of ways you can re-heat pulled meat, including placing the meat in a foil pouch with a tablespoon of unsalted butter. This method allows the meat to effectively steam inside the bag when placed in the oven or barbecue if it is already on.

Other methods can include using the microwave with a piece of paper towel over the meat.

Alternatively, you could try using the quick-fry method in a grill pan with some peanut oil. This is one of my preferred options because I can see and feel the meat cooking in front of me which reduces the chances of it drying out.

Another great tip is to place your leftover pulled rib meat into smaller portioned sealable bags in the freezer to control the amounts you re-heat. Make sure you use a marker to label and date the bags so you can use the oldest portions first.

With most cooked meats stored in the fridge, consume or freeze them within a couple of days for freshest and safest eating.

CHICKEN, CHEESE & CASHEW WOODFIRED PIZZA

Prep Time: 10 minutes & preheat barbecue	Cook Time: 10 minutes	Serves 4	Cooker: Barbecue Smoker	Skill Level: Easy

Method

Preheat a barbecue smoker to 200°C (400°F). Place a pizza stone into the barbecue to warm up over indirect heat.

Mix the sauce ingredients well and apply to the base of the pizza. Top with the pulled chicken rib meat, snow peas, cashews, mozzarella and parmesan.

Cook the pizza over indirect heat on the pizza stone for about 7–10 minutes, or until the cheese has melted and the base is crisp but not too crunchy. Times vary depending on thickness of pizza base.

Tip Add some hot sauce to the barbecue sauce to spice it up to taste.

Ingredients

1 x 15 cm (6-in) pizza base

1 cup pulled chicken rib meat

6 snow peas, sliced

¼ cup cashews

¼ cup grated parmesan cheese

¼ cup grated mozzarella cheese

Sauce

60 ml (2 fl oz) tomato sauce (ketchup)

60 ml (2 fl oz) smoky barbecue sauce

2 garlic cloves, pressed or grated

SMOKED PORK SPRING ROLLS

Prep Time: 20 minutes	Cook Time: 10 minutes	Makes 8 spring rolls	Cooker: Deep-fryer	Skill Level: Easy

Method

Add the pork rib meat, carrots, bean sprouts, snow peas and shallots to a large mixing bowl. Add the hoisin sauce, agave sugar and olive oil. Combine well and set aside.

Preheat a deep-fryer to 180°C (350°F).

Combine all of the sauce ingredients in a small mixing bowl and mix until combined well.

Place 2–3 tablespoons of the pork mixture on the spring roll pastry, roll and fold into a spring roll shape.

Deep-fry the spring rolls, in batches, for 4 minutes, or until golden and crisp. Drain on paper towel.

Serve spring rolls with the dipping sauce.

Tip Replace the pork with chicken or lamb to taste.

Ingredients

300 g (10½ oz) cooked pulled pork rib meat, finely chopped

1 large carrot, finely sliced

½ cup bean sprouts

4 snow peas

¼ cup shallots, finely sliced

1 tablespoon hoisin sauce

1 tablespoon agave sugar

1 tablespoon olive oil

8 spring roll pastry sheets

Sauce

125 ml (4 fl oz) water

juice of 1 lime

1 tablespoon agave sugar

1 tablespoon hoisin sauce

1 teaspoon crushed garlic

½ teaspoon mild chilli powder

SALSA VERDE LAMB BURGER

Prep Time: 15 minutes	Cook Time: 10 minutes	Serves 2	Cooker: Grill Pan & Small Food Processor	Skill Level: Easy

Method

To make the salsa verde, add the coriander, mint, basil and garlic to a small food processor with the olive oil and anchovy and blend until combined and runny. Whilst still processing, add the lime juice, agave sugar and salt and pepper until combined. Remove from the processor and set aside.

Heat the peanut oil in a grill pan over medium heat and add the pulled lamb rib meat. Heat through until serving temperature. Ensure the lamb is still moist and not dry or crunchy.

Add 1 tablespoon Japanese mayonnaise on the base of a bread roll and top with the lamb rib meat. Gently pour the salsa verde over the lamb, to taste. Top with the baby spinach leaves and feta cheese.

Tip Replace the feta cheese with goat's cheese for extra flavor. Replace the lamb rib meat with beef rib meat, if desired.

Ingredients

2 tablespoons of peanut oil
400 g (14 oz) cooked, pulled lamb rib meat
2 tablespoons Japanese mayonnaise
2 crusty bread rolls
8 baby spinach leaves
50 g (1¾ oz) feta cheese, crumbled

Salsa Verde
½ cup chopped parsely
½ cup chopped coriander (cilantro)
½ cup chopped basil
½ cup chopped mint
2 garlic cloves, chopped
185 ml (6 fl oz) olive oil
2 anchovy fillets
juice of 1 lime
1 teaspoon agave sugar
1 teaspoon kosher salt
½ teaspoon freshly cracked black pepper

SPICY APPLE-SLAW PORK SLIDER

Prep Time: 10 minutes	Cook Time: 10 minutes	Serves 2	Cooker: Grill Pan	Skill Level: Easy

Ingredients

2 tablespoons of peanut oil

400 g (14 oz) pulled pork rib meat

2 crusty bread rolls

2 tablespoons smoky barbecue sauce

Slaw

2 large green apples

2 large carrots

¼ red cabbage

3 tablespoons Japanese mayonnaise

1 tablespoon hot sauce

½ teaspoon kosher salt

½ teaspoon freshly cracked black pepper

1 teaspoon agave sugar

Method

In a food processor, finely grate the apples, carrots and red cabbage until consistent in size and consistency. Remove and place in a large mixing bowl. Add the Japanese mayonnaise, hot sauce, salt, pepper and agave sugar and combine thoroughly.

Heat 2 tablespoons of peanut oil in a grill pan and add the pulled pork rib meat. Bring up to serving heat, being careful not to overcook the meat. Should still be moist and tender, not dry or crunchy.

Slice the buns open and add your favorite smoky barbecue sauce to the bottom of the roll. Place the pork directly on top of the sauce, then the apple slaw on top of the pork and close the lid.

Tip Add a squeeze of mild American mustard and two slices of pickles to increase the flavor to taste.

LOW 'N' SLOW BARBECUE PIZZA

Ingredients

1 x 23 cm (9-in) pizza base
60 ml (2 fl oz) barbecue sauce
50 g (1¾ oz) cooked pulled chicken rib
50 g (1¾ oz) cooked pulled pork rib
50 g (1¾ oz) cooked pulled lamb rib
100 g (3½ oz) cooked pulled beef short rib
¼ cup grated mozzarella cheese
¼ cup finely grated parmesan cheese

Prep Time: 10 minutes & Preheat time	Cook Time: 10 minutes	Serves 2	Cooker: Barbecue Smoker	Skill Level: Easy

Method

Preheat a barbecue smoker to 200°C (400°F). Place a pizza stone into the barbecue to warm up over indirect heat.

Apply an even covering of the barbecue sauce to the base of the pizza and top with pulled the chicken, pork, lamb and beef rib meat. Top with the grated mozzarella and parmesan cheese.

Cook the pizza over indirect heat on the pizza stone for about 7–10 minutes, or until the cheese has melted and the base is crisp but not too crunchy. Times vary depending on thickness of pizza base.

Tip Add some hot sauce to the barbecue sauce to spice it up to taste.

GOURMET BEEF NACHOS

Prep Time: 20 minutes	Cook Time: 20 minutes	Serves 4	Cooker: Grill Pan & Oven	Skill Level: Easy

Method

Preheat the oven to 180°C (350°F).

Pull the cooked beef short rib leftovers apart into small chunks and set aside. Discard any bones and/or membrane.

To make the guacamole, add the avocado to a mixing bowl and smash into a chunky paste. Add the red onion, coriander, lime juice, smoked paprika, salt, pepper, agave sugar and chilli powder and combine thoroughly.

On a serving size plate, place a quarter of the corn chips and top with shredded mozzarella cheese and grill in the oven until the cheese has just melted.

Heat 2 tablespoons peanut oil in a grill pan over medium heat and add the pulled beef. Warm through to serving temperature, being careful not to overcook the beef. It should still be soft and moist, not crisp or crunchy.

Add the tomatoes to a mixing bowl with the salt, pepper and olive oil. Mix through and set aside.

To plate, top the corn chips and cheese with the reheated pulled beef, hot sauce, guacamole, diced tomatoes and a dollop of light sour cream. Garnish with chopped coriander and a pinch of smoked paprika.

Ingredients

500 g (17½ oz) pulled beef
375 g (13 oz) unsalted corn chips
200 g (7 oz) shredded mozzarella cheese
2 tablespoons peanut oil
4 tomatoes, finely diced
½ teaspoon freshly cracked black pepper
½ teaspoon kosher salt
50 ml (1¾ fl oz) olive oil
2 tablespoons hot sauce
300 ml (10½ fl oz) low-fat sour cream
¼ cup chopped coriander (cilantro)
½ teaspoon smoked paprika

Guacamole

2 avocados, diced
½ red onion, finely chopped
½ cup finely chopped coriander (cilantro)
juice of 1 lime
1 teaspoon smoked paprika
½ teaspoon freshly cracked black pepper
½ teaspoon kosher salt
½ teaspoon agave sugar
½ teaspoon mild chilli powder

Tip Substitute the beef short rib leftovers for chicken rib, pork rib or lamb rib meat.

AUSSIE LAMB BIG BREAKFAST

Prep Time: 10 minutes	Cook Time: 30 minutes	Serves 4	Cooker: Grill Pan	Skill Level: Easy

Method

Preheat the oven to 180°C (350°F). Double-wrap the cooked pork ribs in foil with 50 g (1¾ oz) of the sliced butter per rack.

Place the ribs, meat side down, in the oven for 15–20 minutes. Remove from the oven and allow to stand for 10 minutes. Unwrap and slice to serve.

Coarsely grate the potatoes into a bowl and mix with 1 egg, kosher salt, cracked pepper, onion powder, garlic powder and smoked paprika. Form into 4 fritter-shaped patties and shallow-fry on each side until crispy and golden, remove from the pan and drain on paper towel.

Fry the mushrooms in a pan with 100 g (3½ oz) of the butter and 2 garlic cloves, stirring occasionally to coat the mushrooms with garlic butter.

Fry the eggs in a separate pan until just cooked and the yolk is runny.

Fry the bacon in a separate pan until crispy, then slice into small pieces.

Combine the bacon and spring onions with 300 ml (10½ fl oz) maple syrup for serving.

Ingredients

2 racks (pre-cooked) lamb ribs

200 g (7 oz) unsalted butter

500 g (1 lb 2 oz) button mushrooms, diced

4 garlic cloves

3 eggs

8 streaky American cut bacon slices

1 spring onion stalk (scallion), finely sliced

300 ml (10½ fl oz) maple syrup

Potato Fritters

300 g (10½ oz) washed baby potatoes

1 egg

1 tablespoon kosher salt

1 teaspoon freshly cracked black pepper

1 teaspoon garlic powder

1 teaspoon onion powder

1 teaspoon smoked paprika

canola oil, for shallow-frying

Tip Serve with your favorite savory barbecue sauce and full strips of bacon instead of maple bacon sauce. Serve with pork ribs for a double pork big breakfast. Substitute potato fritters with Tator Tots if you're short of time.

DOUBLE CHEESE BEEF RIB BURGER

Prep Time: 10 minutes	Cook Time: 10 minutes	Serves 2	Cooker: Grill Pan	Skill Level: Easy

Ingredients

2 tablespoons of peanut oil

400 g (14 oz) cooked pulled beef rib meat

2 blue cheese slices

2 cheddar cheese slices

2 tablespoons smoky barbecue sauce

2 brioche buns, halved

4 slices of pickle

2 teaspoons mild American mustard

2 tablespoons Japanese mayonnaise

Method

Heat the peanut oil in a grill pan over medium heat and add the pulled beef rib meat, placing in two patty-size and shaped portions. Heat the beef through until just warm and add a slice of blue cheese, then cheddar cheese to each of the portions.

Cover the grill pan with a pan lid to steam and melt the cheese onto the beef rib meat. As soon as the cheese has melted onto the beef rib meat, remove and set aside.

Add 1 tablespoon of the smoky barbecue to the base of the brioche roll and top with the re-heated cheesy beef rib meat. Add the pickles, mustard and Japanese mayo on top, to taste, and top with the brioche bun lid.

Tip Substitute the cheddar or blue cheese for your favorite cheese slices. Layer the slices of cheese in between the hot beef to have a lighter melt.

CHIPOTLE LAMB & CORN SALSA SOFT TACOS

Prep Time: 15 minutes	Cook Time: 15 minutes	Serves 2	Cooker: Grill Pan & Small Food Processor	Skill Level: Easy

Method

To make the salsa, add the avocado, white onion, corn kernels, olive oil, salt, pepper and agave sugar to a mixing bowl and mix well. Set aside.

To make the sauce, add the sour cream, chipotle pepper, lime juice, kosher salt and agave sugar to a small food processor and blend to a fine consistency.

Heat the peanut oil in a grill pan over medium heat and add the cooked pulled lamb rib meat. Lightly fry to serving temperature. Ensure the meat is still tender and not dry or crispy. Remove the lamb once at temperature and set aside.

Place the lamb on the taco, drizzle with the chipotle sauce and top with the corn salsa. Add the chopped coriander, to garnish.

Tip Grill the corn on the barbecue to add some smoke and char for extra flavor and visual appeal.

Serve with a Spanish rice for a light meal option. Substitue lamb for beef, pork or chicken.

Ingredients

2 tablespoons peanut oil
300 g (10½ oz) cooked pulled lamb rib meat
4 soft tacos (flour or corn)
½ cup chopped coriander (cilantro)

Salsa

1 avocado, chopped
½ white onion, finely chopped
½ cup corn kernels
2 tablespoons olive oil
½ teaspoon kosher salt
½ teaspoon freshly cracked black pepper
½ teaspoon agave sugar

Sauce

½ cup light sour cream
½ chipotle pepper
juice of ½ lime
¼ teaspoons kosher salt
½ teaspoon agave sugar

CHILLI BEEF BOWL

Prep Time: 10 minutes	Cook Time: 30 minutes	Serves 4	Cooker: Pot	Skill Level: Easy

Ingredients

210 g (7½ oz) red kidney beans
1 red onion, finely chopped
1 tablespoon freshly cracked black pepper
1 tablespoon kosher salt
4 tomatoes, finely chopped
2 tablespoons mild American mustard
1 teaspoon agave sugar
125 ml (4 fl oz) beef stock
2 tablespoons hot sauce
1 small habanero chilli, finely chopped
1 tablespoon Mexican chilli powder
2 garlic cloves, finely chopped
200 g (7 oz) corn chips
100 g (3½ oz) light sour cream
½ cup grated mozzarella cheese
500 g (10½ oz) cooked pulled beef short rib meat
½ cup chopped coriander (cilantro)

Method

In a large pot, all of the ingredients except for the corn chips, sour cream, mozzarella cheese, pulled beef short rib meat and coriander.

Bring the mixture to the boil and simmer for 15 minutes, or until the tomatoes and beans are soft. Stir occasionally to combine and to prevent the bottom of the mixture from overheating.

Add the beef to the chilli mixture and simmer for a further 15 minutes. Remove from the heat to cool slightly before pouring into a large bowl.

Serve with a dollop of light sour cream and mozzarella cheese. Garnish with chopped coriander. Scoop the chilli beef mixture out of the bowl with the corn chips.

. . . .

Tip Add or remove quantity of chilli to taste.

CHICKEN RIB CAESAR BOATS

Prep Time: 15 minutes	Cook Time: 10 minutes	Serves 4	Cooker: Grill Pan & Small Food Processor	Skill Level: Easy

Method

Combine the sauce ingredients in a small mixing bowl and mix well.

In a grill pan over medium heat, add the butter, garlic cloves and bread. Lightly fry the bread cubes, turning often, until crisp and golden on all sides.

In a separate grill pan, add the peanut oil and bacon and lightly fry until just crisp. Drain on paper towel. When cool, roughly chop the bacon.

In a large mixing bowl, combine the pulled chicken, bacon, bread cubes, sauce, parmesan cheese and stir well until combined.

Divide the mixture between 4 lettuce leaves in a boat presentation to serve.

Tip Serve as a light entrée or as a light snack before a main meal. Chop finer or more course to preference.

Ingredients

1 tablespoon peanut oil

4 bacon slices

200 g (7 oz) cooked pulled chicken rib meat

50 g (1¾ oz) unsalted butter

2 garlic cloves

1 cup crusty bread cubes

½ cup finely shaved parmesan cheese

4 cos (romaine) lettuce leaves

Sauce

½ cup Japanese mayonnaise

1 teaspoon mild American mustard

juice of ½ lemon

½ teaspoon kosher salt

½ teaspoon agave sugar

½ teaspoon crushed garlic

¼ teaspoons freshly cracked black pepper

PORK RIB & EGG SPANISH RICE

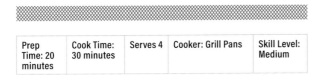

Prep Time: 20 minutes	Cook Time: 30 minutes	Serves 4	Cooker: Grill Pans	Skill Level: Medium

Ingredients

2 racks of cooked pork ribs

2 tablespoons olive oil

½ red onion, finely chopped

2 garlic cloves, finely chopped

300 g (10½ oz) white rice

1 liter (35 fl oz) chicken stock

¼ teaspoon saffron stalks or powder

1 cup diced tomatoes

1 large chorizo sausage, diced

2 tablespoons olive oil

1 squid (calamari) tube, sliced into thin strips

1 large red capsicum (pepper), finely chopped

½ teaspoon kosher salt

1 teaspoon freshly cracked black pepper

1 tablespoon smoked paprika

½ bunch coriander (cilantro)

100 g (3½ oz) unsalted butter

½ cup plain flour

4 eggs

1 cup panko breadcrumbs

Method

Pull the meat from two racks of cooked pork ribs and set aside.

Heat the oil and butter in a pan and add the finely chopped garlic and red onion. Cook until golden.

Add the rice and stir until the rice is fully coated. Slightly brown the rice and slowly add chicken stock, 1 cup at a time, then add the saffron and diced tomatoes. Allow to simmer until the liquid mostly reduced.

In a separate grill pan, shallow-fry the diced chorizo in 2 tablespoons of oil until cooked. Add the pulled pork rib meat and heat through, then set aside.

Coat the squid rings in flour, then egg and then the breadcrumbs and fry until lightly golden.

Add the squid, chorizo and pulled pork rib mix to the rice, with the capsicum, salt and pepper and smoked paprika and combine thoroughly.

Pan-fry the eggs, making sure the yolk is still runny.

Allow the rice to slightly crisp on the bottom of the pan and then stir though the chopped coriander just before serving. Place an egg on top of each portion to serve.

. . . .

Tip Pull the meat from the pork ribs and store in a sealed container in the fridge or freezer while they're still warm as it's easier than pulling the meat off cold ribs.

Add hot sauce or extra chilli to taste to spice it up. Add a runny organic or quail egg on top for something a bit more fancy.

ABOUT THE AUTHOR

Adam Roberts is one of the Co-Founder's of the Australasian Barbecue Alliance and also the General Manager, co-ordinating dozens of wood-fired barbecue competitions across Australia and New Zealand.

Adam regularly competes against Australia's best barbecue teams on the Barbeques Galore Australian Barbecue Championship circuit and has picked up a handful of trophies for various categories including a Reserve Grand Championship trophy in 2017.

With many years of girth-building food experiences or tours of places including the United States, Caribbean, Mexico, South Pacific, Arabian Desert (UAE), Spain, Greece, Italy and Turkey—Adam has picked up some of the best flavor combinations and cooking techniques available and lays them down in *RIBS* for all to enjoy.

Having owned his own mobile food trailer called Yankee Deli, serving American Style Street Food as well as catering functions, food festivals and other events, Adam certainly knows his way around both the indoor and outdoor kitchens.

INDEX

133

ACKNOWLEDGEMENTS

I would like to thank the awesome team at New Holland for the opportunity to publish my first book.

Thanks also to my sensational photographer Sue Stubbs and food stylist Imogene Roache for your help in bringing my recipes to life.

A huge thanks must go to Jay, Louise and Perissa for being great friends who are always willing to sample my recipes and provide valuable feedback on my cook ups.

A big shout out to my home crew, my wifey Kristy, amazing kids Jack and Paige who have endured endless versions of the same recipes over the years in aid of refining and perfecting most of the recipes contained in this book. Thanks for believing in me and all of your support and love.

First published in 2017 by New Holland Publishers
London · Sydney · Auckland

The Chandlery, 50 Westminster Bridge Road, London SE1 7QY, United Kingdom
1/66 Gibbes Street, Chatswood, NSW 2067, Australia
5/39 Woodside Ave, Northcote, Auckland 0627, New Zealand

www.newhollandpublishers.com

A record of this book is held at the British Library and the National Library of Australia.

ISBN: 9781742579566

Group Managing Director: Fiona Schultz
Publisher: Monique Butterworth
Project Editor: Gordana Trifunovic
Proofreader: Kaitlyn Smith
Designer: Andrew Quinlan
Photographer: Sue Stubbs
Stylist: Imogene Roache
Production Director: James Mills-Hicks
Printer: Hang Tai Printing Company Limited

10 9 8 7 6 5 4 3 2 1

Keep up with New Holland Publishers on Facebook
www.facebook.com/NewHollandPublishers